Value-driven Management for International Development and Aid Projects

Firas Izzat Mahmoud Saleh · Noorliza Karia

Value-driven Management for International Development and Aid Projects

Springer

Firas Izzat Mahmoud Saleh
Mercy Corps
Amman, Jordan

Noorliza Karia
School of Management
Universiti Sains Malaysia
Penang, Malaysia

ISBN 978-981-97-3665-2 ISBN 978-981-97-3666-9 (eBook)
https://doi.org/10.1007/978-981-97-3666-9

This Springer imprint is published by the registered company Springer Nature Singapore Pte Ltd.
The registered company address is: 152 Beach Road, #21-01/04 Gateway East, Singapore 189721, Singapore

Noorliza Karia is responsible for editing the content

Contents

Part I
Overview and Strategic Outlook

Chapter 1
Introduction

In the fall of 1982, a six-year-old refugee boy returned to his mother from school with a story to tell. While at school, he had been offered by his teacher a clothing package distributed by the United Nations Relief and Works Agency for Palestine Refugees (UNRWA); however, he refused to accept it, feeling ashamed. His mother, disappointed by his decision, made it clear to him that the neighbor's family needed these clothes and that he should accept the package. This boy is one of the book's authors; who was attending this school in Amman, Jordan, and his grandfather was one of UNRWA's staff 70 years ago.

Since 1948, UNRWA, along with other INGOs, has played an invaluable role in the lives of Palestinian refugees in the Middle East. They have provided food and non-food items, education, healthcare, and employment opportunities to millions of vulnerable people. Despite these decades of efforts and the integration of most of the Palestinian refugees in the hosting communities, there has been a lack of attention given to the quality and accountability standards of international development and aid projects. This has resulted in a lack of sustainability and many of the most vulnerable families being deprived of the support they were intended to receive until today.

Despite the important role played by international non-governmental organizations in saving people and developing marginalized communities since World War II, these organizations have faced criticism related to the managerial and political dynamics of financing and implementing projects. Political dynamics play a significant role in the success of INGOs and their cross-border projects. However, this book focuses on the pragmatic technical lens for managing these projects, prioritizing value-driven approaches in the interest of people of concern.

F. I. Mahmoud Saleh and N. Karia, *Value-driven Management for International Development and Aid Projects*, https://doi.org/10.1007/978-981-97-3666-9_1

1.1 International Non-Governmental Organizations (INGOs)

NGOs are often referred to by a variety of names, including charities, Civic Society Organizations (CSOs), Global Civic Societies (GSCs), Third Sector Organizations (TSOs), Non-Profit Sector (NPOs), Voluntary Organizations (VOs), Civil Society Groups (CSGs), and Community-Based Organizations (CBOs). As Latif and Williams (2017) have noted, these organizations are non-political and neither governmental nor private in nature. Unlike organizations in the private sector, NGOs exist to pursue non-profit objectives and are not directly tied to governmental activities or policies. Lassa (2019) has described NGOs as a special type of non-governmental civil society organization, with a focus on achieving not-for-profit goals.

INGOs, or International Non-Governmental Organizations, are non-profits that operate on an international level to mediate the transfer of resources from developed countries to less developed or crisis-affected countries. Their primary purpose is to provide humanitarian aid, improve people's socio-economic conditions, and assist with post-disaster recovery and rehabilitation. Since the first INGO was founded in 1840, their role in international affairs has grown from providing basic relief items to operating like a government, providing services that governments should but cannot, especially in vulnerable contexts. Today, INGOs are active in the fields of education, healthcare, hygiene, and sanitation, often in the absence of government or when government services are inadequate (Smith 2018).

INGOs strive to address the suffering of people and the vulnerabilities they face worldwide, as well as to promote global Sustainable Development Goals (SDGs). All INGOs are unified by their commitment to upholding human rights, and they are active in times of both peace and armed conflict, as well as in disaster zones and areas in need of humanitarian assistance, development, sustainability, and peacebuilding (Swed 2018).

The Case of the Middle East

In the Middle East, the existence of INGOs is as old as the age of crises and problems in this turbulent region. However, the number of these organizations has increased in an unprecedented manner after 2011, at the beginning of the Syria crisis. Currently, out of 798 INGOs operating in the Middle East and North Africa (MENA) region (Szalai 2018), as of March 2019, 571 organizations are operating in the countries affected by the Syria crisis (Jordan, Lebanon, Turkey, Iraq, Egypt, and Syria) with the UN Economic and Social Council (ECOSOC) Consultative status (UN 2019). Out of those, 270 organizations operate under the Regional Refugee Response Plan (3RP 2019) for the Syrian refugee crisis. To that end, they implemented their IDAPs to respond to the affected people in five countries hosting Syrian refugees.

1.2 International Development and Aid Projects (IDAPs)

Regardless of their aim, most INGOs operate using project-based organizational structures. This allows these organizations to deliver support and services to their targeted groups in a more controllable and measurable way (Martinez and Cooper 2017). International Development and Aid Projects (IDAPs) are initiatives implemented by international entities such as UN agencies, international organizations, or INGOs in contexts that are either vulnerable or unstable. These contexts could include areas affected by natural disasters, man-made crises, or underdeveloped countries.

Common work settings for IDAPs include refugee camps, informal settlements, urban areas, war zones, and remotely managed areas. INGOs authorize IDAPs to provide necessary social services such as potable water and sanitation, education, and helping communities suffering from infectious diseases (PMI 2017). They also focus on achieving the SDGs to address global challenges like poverty, inequality, environmental degradation, climate change, peace and justice, and prosperity.

The range of activities for IDAPs varies, depending on the context, and can include responding to people displacement, poverty alleviation, promotion of human rights, post-disaster recovery, reconstruction, and restoration, emergency and humanitarian aid, response to rural–urban and climate-induced migrations, education of global citizenship and integration of immigrants, educational development, food security, agricultural education and training, urban development, sport for development and peace, water management, electricity and energy, community self-reliance and institutional governance, early childhood, child protection, and family-based care, protection of cultural heritage, or reproductive health development.

In contrast to traditional approaches that focus solely on lifesaving interventions, modern aid projects encompass activities from both tangible and intangible support, including long-term development activities such as building governmental and institutional systems (McEvoy et al. 2016). However, aid projects and long-term development projects are generally treated separately in the literature (Golini et al. 2015).

Case of the Protracted Refugee Crisis

The 3RP, an umbrella of projects in response to the Syrian crisis, includes both aid projects and development projects. This "Nexus Approach" bridges the gap between humanitarian and long-term interventions and is accepted by all involved as a viable solution for this ongoing crisis. This comprehensive approach is referred to as International Development and Aid Projects (IDAPs). The figure below shows Palestinian refugees who were internally displaced in Yarmouk Camp, Syria. These individuals had initially relocated to Syria as refugees from the Arab–Israeli War in 1948, only to become refugees again during the Syrian crisis, highlighting the precariousness and multifaceted nature of the refugee crises that have arisen in the Middle East.

The Crisis in Yarmouk Camp. *Source* https://www.unrwa.org/crisis-in-yarmouk.

1.3 Why This Book?

The INGOs sector has seen significant expansion in recent years in response to an increase in natural disasters and man-made crises, as well as the rising levels of poverty and inequality the world over. These organizations are viewed by many, in combination with the private and governmental sectors, as a powerful force for positive change in the global domain. Their primary goal is to provide humanitarian aid and promote social and economic development for those affected by these crises.

INGOs are organizations that are measured by the success of their strategic plans, which are implemented and managed through individual IDAPs. To ensure that these projects yield maximum value and efficiency, Project Management (PM) tools are employed. Evidence has demonstrated that the use of PM strategies can increase the success of projects and strengthen the competition for funding. However, it is necessary to make contextual adjustments to standard PM models for each sector to ensure their effectiveness and add value to the lives of affected people.

This book has been motivated by the numerous tragedies that have occurred around the globe, in which sustainability and lasting impact have not been achieved for the people affected by the crisis. It provides readers with value-driven PM disciplines for IDAPs, which will aid in better management of these projects, ultimately resulting in a more beneficial outcome for disadvantaged and crisis-affected individuals.

Under the umbrella of human rights, INGOs are tasked with implementing a variety of IDAPs. These projects, mainly funded by international donors, have superior humanitarian goals and SDGs for people and developing countries (Ayoyo 2019). By undertaking these projects, INGOs are attempting to protect at-risk individuals, meet their needs, enhance their resilience, and empower them, as well as develop their communities socially and economically with a focus on sustainability, peace-building, and improving the quality of life for them and future generations (Walton 2018).

As liaisons between international donors and domestic stakeholders, INGOs must maintain all directions of accountability when implementing their projects (Berghmans et al. 2017; Aldashev and Navarra 2018). This includes meeting the expectations of donors for efficiency and recipients for effectiveness. Through their role, INGOs ensure that vital services reach vulnerable people and that all stakeholders are held accountable.

Despite their importance to crisis-affected communities, INGOs have had difficulty attaining their goals and satisfying the needs of people through their IDAPs. The World Bank (Yamin and Sim 2016) and (Latif and Williams 2017) have reported high levels of failure in IDAPs. Furthermore, these projects have not been able to demonstrate a significant and lasting impact on vulnerable and crisis-affected people's lives, nor have they been supported enough by donors. Saleh et al. (2017) report similar empirical findings, with respondents ranking "*Our Interventions Provide Sustainability for the Beneficiaries*" as the lowest performance indicator for their projects. These projects are further hindered by a lack of inclusion of beneficiaries, providing relevant services, and efficiency (Voluntas 2018; Hemsley and Achilles 2019). Unfortunately, this issue has been compounded by decreasing funds from donors, leading to increased competition among INGOs to secure financing for their projects (Nanthagopan et al. 2019).

It has been widely acknowledged that an effective performance-driven PM is absent from projects of this type. This has led to a gap between the desired superior goals of IDAPs and their actual outcomes, which is often attributed to the lack of adoption of good performance PM for this sector (Frimpong and Oluwoye 2018) or the inability of standard PM models to meet the specific needs of IDAPs and to address the complex realities of these projects (Steinfort 2010; Ika and Hodgson (2014); Golini et al. 2015; Golini et al. 2017, Matos et al. 2019). Consequently, there is a recurring call to advance PM theory and practices to optimize the performance of IDAPs (Landoni and Corti 2011; Golini et al. 2016; Steinfort 2017; Matos et al. 2019). This would increase the probability of success of the projects, maximize their social impact (Golini and Landoni 2014), and boost the competitive position of INGOs in the acquisition of donor funds (Lacruz and Cunha 2018). Additionally, it would enhance the trust of all involved stakeholders in these vital projects (Arhin et al. 2018). With the emergence of the COVID-19 pandemic, this need has been further emphasized, as IDAPs can be susceptible to sudden stoppages and disconnections from the target population (Saleh and Karia 2020).

To that end, this book articulates the relevant published research efforts, the authors' research, and their practical experience as practitioners in the INGOs industry in ten chapters to provide audiences with a firsthand experience needed to manage IDAPs in a way that adds value to the lives of crisis-affected people. These chapters are grouped into two parts.

Part I sheds light on the need for a new paradigm and lays the strategic foundation for value-driven management of IDAPs (Chapter 2), unpacks the complexities of IDAPs (Chapter 3), explores the different dimensions of strategic alignments of IDAPs (Chapter 4), and finally, it discusses the different preparations required to ensure value-driven design and fundraising for IDAPs (Chapter 5). Part II, however, includes six chapters to delve into the core elements of managing IDAPs, consisting of the management of people of concern, targeted communities, and partners (Chapter 6), the management of monitoring, evaluation, accountability, and learning (Chapter 7), the management of advocacy and communication with communities (Chapter 8), the management of social workers and resources (Chapter 9), the management of donors (Chapter 10), and lastly, the management of information for the new normal and sustainability (Chapter 11).

References

Aldashev G, Navarra C (2018) Development NGOs: basic facts. Ann Public Coop Econ 89(1):125–155

Arhin AA, Kumi E, Adam MAS (2018) Facing the bullet? Non-governmental organizations' (NGOs') responses to the changing aid landscape in Ghana. VOLUNTAS: Int J Volunt Nonprofit Organ 29(2):348–360

Ayoyo DD (2019) INGOs/IGOs and the diffusion of human rights: practices, prospects, and perils. Soc Mov Stud 18(3):381–384

Berghmans M, Simons M, Vandenabeele J (2017) What is negotiated in negotiated accountability? The case of INGOs. VOLUNTAS: Int J Volunt Nonprofit Organ 28(4):1529–1561

Frimpong Y, Oluwoye J (2018) Project management practice in groundwater construction project in Ghana. Am J Manag Sci Eng 3(5):60–68

Golini R, Landoni P (2014) International development projects by non-governmental organizations: an evaluation of the need for specific project management and appraisal tools. Impact Assess Proj Apprais 32(2):121–135

Golini R, Corti B, Landoni P (2016) More efficient project execution and evaluation with logical framework and project cycle management: evidence from international development projects. Impact Assess Proj Apprais 35(2):128–138

Golini R, Kalchschmidt M, Landoni P (2015) Adoption of project management practices: the impact on international development projects of non-governmental organizations. Int J Project Manage 33(3):650–663

Golini R, Landoni P, Kalchschmidt M (2017) The adoption of the logical framework in international development projects: a survey of non-governmental organizations. Impact Assess Proj Apprais 36(2):145–154

Hemsley M, Achilles K (2019) Aid in Limbo: why Syrians deserve support to rebuild their lives. Oxfam Library

Ika LA, Hodgson D (2014) Learning from international development projects: blending critical project studies and critical development studies. Int J Project Manage 32(7):1182–1196

Lacruz A, Cunha E (2018) Project management office in non-governmental organizations: an ex post facto study. Revista De Gestão 25(2):212–227

Landoni P, Corti B (2011) The management of international development projects: moving toward a standard approach or differentiation? Proj Manag J 42(3):45–61

Lassa JA (2019) Roles of non-government organizations in disaster risk reduction. Oxford Research Encyclopedia of Natural Hazard Science

Latif KF, Williams N (2017) Team effectiveness in non-governmental organizations (NGOs) projects. Eval Program Plann 64:20–32

Martinez DE, Cooper DJ (2017) Assembling international development: accountability and the disarticulation of a social movement. Acc Organ Soc 63:6–20

Matos PV, Romão M, Sarmento JM, Abaladas A (2019) The adoption of project management methodologies and tools by NGDOs: a mixed methods perspective. J Bus Res 101:651–659

McEvoy P, Brady M, Munck R (2016) Capacity development through international projects: a complex adaptive systems perspective. Int J Manag Proj Bus 9(3):528–545

Nanthagopan Y, Williams N, Thompson K (2019) Levels and interconnections of project success in development projects by non-governmental organizations (NGOs). Int J Manag Proj Bus 12(2):487–511

Project Management Institute (PMI) (2017) Project management body of knowledge (PMBOK® Guide). Project Management Institute Inc., PA

Regional Refugee and Resilience Plan (2019) Regional Strategic Overview 2019/2020

Saleh FIM, Sweis RJ, Abdelqader BY, Abdallah AB, Arafeh M (2017) The effect of TQM dimensions on the performance of international non-governmental organizations operating in Jordan. Int J Prod Qual Manag 21(4):443–459

Saleh FIM, Karia N (2020) Benchmarks for INGOs' effective responses during COVID-19 pandemic. Benchmarking: Int J 27(10):2863–2886

Smith AN (2018) Foreign aid and development in the Democratic Republic of the Congo: an analysis of international barriers to development. Perceptions 4(2):19–19

Steinfort P (2010) Understanding the antecedents of project management best practice—Lessons to be learned for and from aid/relief projects. Dissertation. https://researchbank.rmit.edu.au/eserv/rmit:7526/Steinfort.pdf

Steinfort P (2017) Community and post-disaster program management methodology. Int J Project Manage 35(5):788–801

Swed O (2018) Promoting human rights under fire: INGOs' mitigating effect on human rights violations during armed conflict. Soc Sci Res 75:1–2

Szalai M (2018) The International NGO triangle on the mena region. MENARA Working Papers, Middle East and North Africa regional architecture: mapping geopolitical shifts, regional order and domestic transformations. Accessed from https://www.iai.it/sites/default/files/menara_wp_19.pdf.

Voluntas (2018) State of the Syria crisis response: assessing humanitarian and development challenges. Voluntas, Second annual report. https://reliefweb.int/report/syrian-arab-republic/state-syria-crisis-response-assessing-humanitarian-and-development

Walton O (2018) Beyond disaster framing: exploring multi-mandate INGOs' representations of conflict. Third World Q 39(4):642–660

Yamin M, Sim AKS (2016) Critical success factors for international development projects in Maldives. Int J Manag Proj Bus 9(3):481–504

Chapter 2
The Need for a New Paradigm

2.1 Introduction

For the past few decades, the global development paradigm has been rapidly shifting due to the anti-globalization movement and the rise of nationalism. This has been heavily influenced by the changing power dynamics, unifications, and divisions across the globe. As a result, academics and practitioners alike have begun to question the forms and methods of international development funding and implementation.

Ika and Hodgson (2014) trace the evolution of PM approaches in the international development arena over the last six decades, beginning with traditional approaches and progressing to include contingent approaches before culminating in the critical approaches that assess international development projects through the lenses of post-development, Habermasian, Foucauldian, and Neo-Marxist theories.

In 2016, the World Humanitarian Summit brought about the creation of the "*Grand Bargain*" Agreement, in which all international actors committed to ten goals in order to increase coordination, reduce duplication, and improve joint assessments and participation. This agreement aimed to harmonize reporting, promote localization, and emphasize engagement between humanitarian and development organizations (Hilhorst et al. 2019).

Over the last ten years, there has been a consensus that localization should be taken into account when it comes to international development and aid. This has shifted the traditional approach to project management success, which is often measured solely by its ultimate impact and sustainability on those affected by the crisis, and instead emphasized the role of community leadership and those who are in need.

F. I. Mahmoud Saleh and N. Karia, *Value-driven Management for International Development and Aid Projects*, https://doi.org/10.1007/978-981-97-3666-9_2

2.2 Expectations of People

The complexity of IDAPs is highlighted by the mediating role of INGOs, which creates an imbalance of power between donors and implementers of these projects on one side and the targeted people and communities on the other. This power imbalance is often perceived by recipients of aid and development as hostile and advancing the donor's agenda. This is particularly true in fragile, corrupted contexts and is often linked to the poor performance of IDAPs. This has led to criticism of IDAPs and has demonstrated the need to set people's expectations and commit to greater accountability (Jamal and Baldwin 2019; Boomsma and O'Dwyer 2019). Thus, being accountable to people and setting their expectations must be a key factor in the success of IDAPs.

When INGOs experience a shortage of funds and resources, stakeholders tend to place higher expectations on them for accountability (AbouAssi and Makhlouf 2018). Ika and Saint-Macary (2012) suggest that this lack of resources might lead INGOs to prioritize up-accountability (i.e., accountability to donors) over down-accountability (i.e., accountability to service recipients or targeted communities) and potentially weaken beneficiary-focused accountability mechanisms, as Yasmin and Ghafran (2019) have discussed. Additionally, INGOs often enforce the views and priorities of their donors when considering the needs of communities, which can lead to non-needs-based interventions (Aldashev and Navarra 2018) and reduce the decision-making power of the targeted groups (Penn 2019).

In order to put people at the center of humanitarian and development interventions, various initiatives and industry-specific frameworks have been established and adopted by INGOs. Of these, the Sphere Project is widely recognized as the oldest initiative in the humanitarian standards field, first tested in 1997 and now known as the Sphere Handbook 2018. This handbook emphasizes the need for a rights-based approach, including the rights of people to be assisted, to live with dignity, to be secure and protected, and to participate and have a decision-making role in their own recovery (Sphere Project 2019a).

In 2008, ten leading INGOs founded the Accountability Charter initiative to strengthen their collective voice of accountability. This has since been renamed Accountable Now and consists of 26 INGOs, who define accountability as "*being transparent on what the organization is, what it commits to doing, and progress achieved; engaging key stakeholders in meaningful dialogue to enable continuous improvement for those we serve; using power responsibly; and enabling stakeholders to hold us to account effectively*" (Accountable Now 2019). Additionally, these organizations have agreed on ten commitments, including Respect for Human Rights, Independence, Transparency, Good Governance, Responsible Advocacy, Participation, Diversity/Inclusion, Environmental Responsibility, Ethical Fundraising, and Professional Management (Crack 2018; Accountable Now 2019).

Since that time, the International Red Cross and Red Crescent Movement and NGOs in Disaster Relief have developed a number of industry-specific initiatives such as the Code of Conduct, People in Aid, the Active Learning Network for Accountability and Performance in Humanitarian Action (ALNAP), and the Humanitarian Accountability Partnership (HAP). Sweis et al. (2016) and Sanderson (2017) have reviewed these initiatives, yet INGOs still have difficulty ensuring accountability and trust with the target communities. This lack of trust has hindered the success of their IDAPs, particularly those that include social-related activities (Jamal and Baldwin 2019). In response to this, the Core Humanitarian Standards on Quality and Accountability (CHS) were presented in 2014 to replace Sphere's Core Standards (Sphere Project 2019b). CHS is unique in its alignment with Total Quality Management (TQM) concepts, such as the industry-specific TQM dimensions identified by Sweis et al. (2016) and it emphasizes on putting the beneficiaries at the center of relief efforts (Robehmed 2019).

Currently, the CHS Alliance is an organization of more than 200 agencies striving to ensure the highest quality and accountability of international aid and development assistance provided to crisis-affected people (Hilhorst 2015). According to the Sphere Project (2019a), individuals and organizations involved in humanitarian and development work can use the Nine Commitments as a standard. These commitments are: (1) "*The humanitarian response is appropriate and relevant*"; (2) "*The humanitarian response is effective and timely*"; (3) "*The humanitarian response strengthens local capacities and avoids negative effects*"; (4) "The humanitarian response is based on communication, participation, and feedback"; (5) "*Complaints are welcomed and addressed*"; (6) "*The humanitarian response is coordinated and complementary*"; (7) "The humanitarian actors continuously learn and improve"; (8) "The humanitarian staff are supported to do their job effectively, and everyone is treated fairly"; and (9) "*Resources are managed and used responsibly for their intended purpose*" (Sanderson 2017). As illustrated in Fig. 2.1.

The verification process of CHS (2019) revealed that the lowest performance average scores within the sector were for commitment numbers 5, 4, and 7. Commitment 5, "*complaints are welcomed and addressed,*" scored 2.1 out of 5, Commitment 4, "*The humanitarian response is based on communication, participation, and feedback,*" scored 2.5 out of 5, and Commitment 7, "*The humanitarian actors continuously learn and improve,*" scored 2.5 out of 5. Thus, two of the weakest commitments with respect to performance average were associated with people's participation and satisfaction, while the third commitment pertained to continuous improvement. This, however, CHS, which has developed by the sector for the sector:

> places communities and people affected by crisis at the centre of humanitarian action. (Sphere Project 2019a)

The risk of excluding communities in decision-making can have dire consequences, such as direct exclusion of their needs, similar to the case of for-profits when dealing with customers (Sweis et al. 2016). This has led to the wide adoption of a community-based approach that puts people's voices at the forefront, addresses their needs, and increases their resilience (Shaw 2016; Lassa 2019). To this end, CARE International (2017) published their "*She is Humanitarian*" report, providing evidence from Jordan and the Philippines that women can play a major role in *"places communities and people affected by crisis at the centre of humanitarian action"* Sphere Project (2019a).

Fig. 2.1 Core Humanitarian Standards (CHS) (*Source* CHS [2019])

responding to conflicts and disasters rather than just being victims or recipients of aid. Rahman (2018) discussed the role of the community in managing disasters and risk reduction in Malaysia, while Sawchuk (2018) explored ActionAid's Rights-Based Approach and localization agenda in the Pacific, which seeks to catalyze local gender responses and reduce the dependence on INGOs. Fox (2018) suggested that public accountability terms, like right-to-know, transparency, and advocacy, should be communicated with local communities in a way that is sensitive to domestic cultures. In order to build trust with communities, INGOs should create a space for listening to their voices, learning from them, respecting their culture and religion, engaging stakeholders in decision-making, committing to long-term presence, and ensuring transparency (Jamal and Baldwin 2019).

INGOs should institutionalize a community-based approach to participation, including all parts of the target communities, rather than an ad-hoc or project-based approach. Scholars have offered several modalities for participation, which can be manifested in various forms. These include early consultations with communities to ensure their involvement in the design of IDAPs, the proactive engagement of communities in implementation, and after-the-fact consultations. Moreover, honest and timely information should be shared with communities, and safe, formal, and accessible feedback and accountability mechanisms should be provided (Opdyke et al. 2018; Sweis et al. 2016). Additionally, "*community representatives*" should be included in the project planning process, so that their feedback can be taken into account as projects are tailored to meet their needs (Davis and Garb 2019).

2.3 Linkage with the Broader Structures and Programs

Projects cannot be implemented in a vacuum; this is especially true when taking into account the external enterprise environmental factors of the implementation context (PMI 2017) and the organization's environment. As such, the predominant view of PM literature, which concentrates on individual projects, may not be sufficient or practical, according to Ika (2012). In contrast, the organizational elements of implementing organizations must be considered and managed by the IDAPs.

IDAPs may encounter three types of problems connected to the success of the project. The first of these are "*Structural/Contextual Problems*," which arise from the external environment, such as PESTEL analysis (Political, Economic, Social, Technological, Environmental, and Legal). The second, "*Institutional/Sustainability Problems*," refers to the lack of institutional capacity to implement and deliver sustainable outcomes. The third, "*Managerial/Organizational Problems*," relates to the direct managerial aspects of the project, e.g., the PM itself (Ika 2012). Ika and Donnelly (2017) have identified these problems as conditions for project success, and they are widely accepted by both scholars and practitioners. Levie et al. (2017) have emphasized the importance of managing the complexity of IDAPs, while McEvoy et al. (2016) and Steinfort (2017) have stressed the need to link the project with longer-term governance structures for improved impact evaluation and sustainability.

INGOs often use donor-funded projects to achieve their strategic missions. As such, the connection between organizational development and PM is increasingly important. Development in organizational aspects can lead to continuous learning, building organizational knowledge, and more effective management of IDAPs (McEvoy et al. 2016). Yamin and Sim (2016) view the institutional environment as a critical success factor for IDAPs, which has been discussed in several research studies on "*Governance*" (Omar and Ismail 2019). Levie et al. (2017) also concluded that project governance is essential in bridging the gap between PM and corporate governance and in post-conflict scenarios.

Projects are not only designed to contribute to the strategic and business plans of INGOs but also work as part of larger social, market, and political systems. Programs and portfolios are designed for longer-term benefits (McEvoy et al. 2016; Steinfort 2017). Senior management teams and other functions within the INGO are involved in IDAPs rather than the project manager or team alone (Levie et al. 2017).

This book aims to use an organizational management approach namely the Total Quality Management to assess or verify the standard PM methodologies used by INGOs to better manage and sustain projects (Saleh and Karia 2020).

Total Quality Management (TQM) has been widely lauded as a holistic management philosophy (Gomes et al. 2019) and a widely adopted organizational approach (Altayeb and Alhasanat 2014). It is a popular choice for organizations aiming to compete domestically and globally (Bouranta et al. 2019). Additionally, TQM is favored by organizations that need to be agile in delivering services to their customers (Rohaizan and Tan 2011). At the core of this approach lies organizational culture, which necessitates the involvement of all members of the organization to achieve excellence (Salah and Rahim 2019).

TQM is a management philosophy that has become increasingly popular as a means of improving organizational productivity and quality. It has been described using a variety of terms, such as "*total quality control*," "*total quality leadership*," "*continuous quality improvement*," and "total quality improvement program." At its core, TQM is a collaborative system that involves all stakeholders in taking responsibility for improving quality within an organization (Karia and Saleh 2021). The three primary components of TQM are quality, client satisfaction, and continuous improvement.

Within organizations, TQM authority oversees the day-to-day quality improvement operations. To achieve this, multiple improvement teams are established to manage individual TQM tasks. However, the authority of TQM varies between organizations. Numerous global excellence models are used to govern TQM, including the European Foundation for Quality Management (EFQM).

Total TQM, a modern management approach (PMI 2017), illustrates the progressive evolution of the term "*Quality*." This development has been through the stages of inspection, control quality, and assurance quality (Sweis et al. 2016). Consequently, the emergence of TQM has been accompanied by the expansion of the definition of the term "*Quality*." Although there is no consensus on a single definition, it is said that "*Quality is in the eye of the beholder*" (Van Kemenade and Hardjono 2019).

TQM is an approach to quality that starts with perfect design (Taguchi's Perspective), leading to high-quality results. Quality is an essential part of the mission and vision of INGO and is strategically pursued (Deming's Perspective). To ensure the successful implementation of TQM, the organizational culture must be supportive, staff must be empowered, and feedback from staff and clients must be welcome (Rani 2018).

Van Kemenade and Hardjono (2019) have identified four paradigms of TQM, each with its own definition of quality, objectives, focus, and tools. Table 2.1 in their article summarizes these paradigms and describes the historical evolution of TQM to the "*Emergence Paradigm*" or TQM of the twenty-first century. This approach requires organizations to be flexible and responsive to their context and to include all stakeholders, while also communicating core values, displaying supportive leadership, and having a positive organizational culture (Van Kemenade and Hardjono 2019).

Table 2.1 Total quality management in four paradigms

	Empirical paradigm	Reference paradigm	Reflective paradigm	Emergence paradigm
Quality is	Conformance to requirements	Quality is fitness for use	Quality is subjective	Quality is not static, but dynamic
Adage	"To measure is to know"	"We need to improve continuously"	"Quality is not a thing, it is an event"	"The truth is what works"
Focus	Rules, standards	Models, guidelines	Principles	Shared values, virtues
Aim	Control	Improvement	Professionalism	Flexibility
Problem	The unpredictability of product and uncontrollability of processes	Sub-optimizations	Insufficient self-criticism	Inability to cope with changes
Solution	Take causes of variation away	PDCA cycle	Detaching mechanisms	Adjusting to the context, breakthrough
Tools	SPC Seven tools Six Sigma Joint Commission International Accreditation Evidence-based medicine, Protocols	ISO9000-series EFQM-model Malcolm Baldrige Award Quality circles	The second opinion, Inter-vision, Time out, Discussion Stories Inner conversations, Shadowing, Modeling, peer review	Context analysis, Quality circles ACCRA© Lean Appreciative Inquiry Socratic café
Friedson (2001)	Manager in lead	Customer in lead	Professional in lead	All stakeholders

Source Adapted from Van Kemenade and Hardjono (2019)

The "*Emergence Paradigm*" of TQM is most suitable for INGOs, as the business environment is characterized by uncertainty and intangibility and involves diverse stakeholders. Sweis et al. (2016) developed a TQM Benchmarking Model for INGOs based on a comprehensive literature review, as depicted in Fig. 2.2. This model was tested by Saleh et al. (2017) in the context of INGOs operating in response to the Syrian crisis in Jordan and was found to have a 58.8% influence on the performance of these organizations. The greatest contribution was attributed to leadership and management commitment, beneficiary focus and participation, partnership management for sustainability, and the use of quality information. Mahmoud et al. (2019) subsequently validated the TQM Benchmarking Model in the Middle East, confirming the six dimensions of the model.

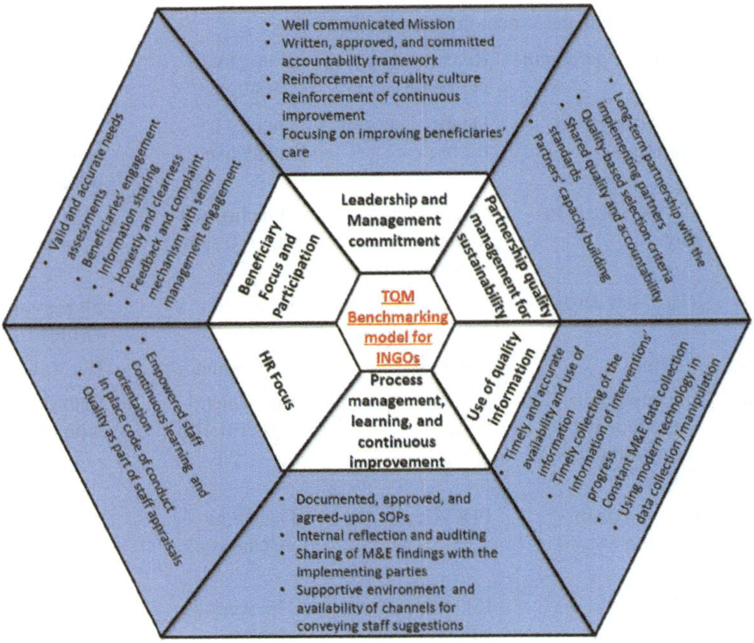

Fig. 2.2 TQM benchmarking model (*Source* Sweis et al. [2016])

2.4 Current Approaches and Standards for Managing IDAPs

PM is a business process that provides organizations with the tools and strategies to implement projects efficiently and effectively and maintain their competitiveness and business value. This view is the common view in the literature, though some researchers have separated their views of PM into two perspectives: the "*rationale view.*" which focuses on specific processes, policies, and rules; and the "*resource-based*" or "*behavioral view*," which emphasizes people-based aspects (Nanthagopan et al. 2019). Combining both views can lead to improved performance, contribute to managing complexity, uncertainty, and sustainability in projects, and increase the chances of project success (Yao 2016).

Standard PM models are the traditional embodiments of the "*systematic*," "*rational*," or "*technically based*" irreplaceable view of PM. These models strive to provide processes, tools, and techniques to increase the precision of projects, helping to avoid delays and higher costs (Rehacek 2017; Alves and Gonçalves 2018).

Despite the potential correlation between the standard PM models and the performance of IDAPs, there were numerous opinions and empirical reports in the literature that led to the question of which standard to adopt. This could be seen as a logical reflection of the multiplicity of PM models and methodologies. While literature was lacking when it came to PM models specifically for the IDAPs, PM "*methodology*," as described by Golini and Landoni (2014), could be in the form of general standards such as the Project Management Body of Knowledge (PMBOK® Guide) and International Project Management Association (IPMA), or those specifically developed for the IDAPs and NGOs sector in general, such as PM4DEV, PM4NGOs, and Logical Framework (Lacruz and Cunha 2018).

The PMBOK® Guide, as a general PM Standard, describes itself as a set of widely applied and innovative practices that are progressively emerging as the knowledge of the PM profession and have been established as a "*good practice*," that has evolved constantly (PMI 2017). Additionally, the PMBOK® Guide has been identified as a guidebook of methods and processes needed to successfully deliver the planned and timely outputs within the cost and quality standards, while some have regarded it as the most adopted PM Standard (Keleckaite and Meiliene 2015). Most organizations build their own methodologies based on the PMBOK® Guide. In addition to the PMBOK® Guide, IPMA, PRINCE2, ISO 9000, and Project Cycle Management (PCM) have also been acknowledged by scholars and practitioners as valid "methodologies" in the various contexts of the IDAPs.

The literature is in agreement that PM has severe theoretical shortcomings (Lousberg 2006; Abd Elhameed 2018). Koskela and Howell (2002) suggested that the PM theory can be divided into the theory of project and the theory of management. The theory of project is based on the transformation theory from operations management, while the theory of management is grounded in the theories of management-as-planning (planning), classical communication theory (execution), and thermostat theory (control).

The last two decades have seen a shift in the literature toward the "soft" side of PM; managing human processes and the "*soft side*" of PM (Pollack 2007), and the recognition of political activities as a core part of PM (Lousberg 2006). The PMBOK® Guide has been linked to various theories, including leadership theory, the resource-based view of the firm theory, temporary organization theory, knowledge flow theory, and queuing theory (Abd Elhameed 2018), in an attempt to provide theoretical justification for the academic community. Kwak and Anbari (2009) conducted a systematic literature review and concluded that PM is more of an applied field than a distinct academic discipline, leading to a pessimistic outlook regarding its theoretical justification.

The PMBOK® Guide has evolved and grown over time, incorporating a wide variety of theoretical foundations that are reflected in its knowledge areas. It has become the accepted body of knowledge, theoretical framework, and foundation for PM, developed through firsthand observations of practitioners rather than academics (Abd Elhameed 2018; Baker 2018). Through this book, we provide a firsthand, complementary view of the PMBOK® Guide and offer a way to ensure value-driven management of IDAPs.

Hermano et al. (2013) have proposed PMDPro1 as an alternative, more efficient approach than the "*Logical Framework*" for managing development projects. Other scholars have suggested that Result-Based Management could replace the "*Logical Framework*," which has success criteria as well as an approximate cost and timeline. Furthermore, PMDPro1 and PM4DEV have been perceived by practitioners as

Table 2.2 The processes included in the guidelines

Project management disciplines	PMBOK	PMDPro1	PM4DEV
Project Scope Management	Yes	Yes	Yes
Project Time Management	Yes	Yes	Yes
Project Cost Management	Yes	Yes	Yes
Project Risk Management	Yes	Yes	Yes
Project Human Resource Management	Yes	Yes	Yes
Project Stakeholders Management	Yes	Yes	Yes
Project Integration Management	Yes	–	–
Project Quality Management	Yes	–	Yes
Project Communication Management	Yes	–	Yes
Project Procurement Management	Yes	Yes	Yes
Project Justification Management	–	Yes	–

Source Golini and Landoni (2014)

viable options for the international standard PM models such as the PMBOK® Guide (Golini et al. 2015). To further explore this, Golini and Landoni (2014) conducted a comparison among PMBOK® Guide, PMDPro1, and PM4DEV, excluding the IPMA as a benchmark. Table 2.2 displays the comparison of the three methodologies in terms of PM processes. The outcome of this analysis demonstrated that the PMBOK® Guide is the most complete standard. Nevertheless, because of its generalizability, it is missing some industry-specific tools like "*Logical Framework*" which are included in PMDPro1, and other industry-specific management tools. Therefore, despite their focus on international development rather than aid projects, Golini and Landoni (2014) suggested integrating industry-specific aspects with standard PM models as a potential area of PM research within the sector. However, this is a daunting task due to the reported limitations of existing PM models in their original forms and the complexity of IDAPs, as highlighted by Vahanvati and Mulligan (2017).

2.5 Deficiencies of Standard PMBOK® Guide

PMI's inclination toward adapting the standard PMBOK® Guide does not guarantee that it is suitable for INGOs. Adjustments may need to go beyond the mere use of templates, inputs, tools, and techniques, and even require the development of new domains or processes (Anderson and Lannon 2018). This is because the overall approach of PM may have to be altered in order to meet the individual needs of a particular crisis (Howsawi et al. 2014).

As part of Steinfort's funded Ph.D. through the PMI, Steinfort and Walker (2007, 2008), Steinfort (2010), and Steinfort (2017) have critiqued the PMI's methodology with regard to post-disaster reconstruction projects. As a result, he offered three key suggestions. First, he suggested that PMI methodology should take into account "*culturally centric programs of projects/work.*" This requires addressing program and portfolio management issues for the benefit of all parties. His second point was that NGOs should encourage their donors to support the establishment of PMOs and other governance structures to cultivate the organization's PM competencies and overall quality, effectiveness, and outcomes. Finally, he proposed broadening the appreciation of project governance tools, citing the PMBOK® Guide as an example of a tool that does not meet the specific needs of the INGOs sector, such as Monitoring and Evaluation (M&E) and Logical Framework. Steinfort also made the point that the tools and techniques of PM would not be successful if they did not consider the cultural context of implementation. He also noted that multiple political and community aspects should be considered. To conclude, he suggested that ensuring the survival of affected people and the sustainability of social development requires considering the PM processes within the larger vision, objectives, programs, performance criteria, and governance structures, as advocated by McEvoy et al. (2016).

Recently, Hermano and Martín-Cruz (2019) have argued that uncertain and dynamic environments necessitate viewing the PMBOK® Guide through a dynamic lens. As such, they identified candidate processes that could be suitable for such environments, such as Monitor and Control Project Work, Perform Integrated Change Control, Verify Scope, Control Scope, Control Schedule, Control Costs, Perform Quality Control, Manage Stakeholders' Expectations, and Risk Management Processes. Nevertheless, AbouAssi and Makhlouf (2018) contended that INGOs tend to employ standard PM models even if they have not been explicitly declared or formally recognized. Moreover, the two issues still need to be acknowledged, defined, and labeled, requiring adaptation while keeping their IDAPs flexible, innovative, transformative, and creative. According to PMI (2017), tailoring should be based on the project's complexity and application area. Thus, the standard PM model needs to be verified and adapted for IDAPs implemented by INGOs. The limitations of standard PM practices may lead to impediments to success and even result in failure (McEvoy et al. 2016), which this study is attempting to address in its context.

Despite the agreed-upon benefits of PM for IDAPs (Dumrak et al. 2017) and various adaptation attempts, there is no evidence of a significant application of PM models within this sector (Keleckaite and Meiliene 2015). Keleckaite and Meiliene (2015) found that the absence of PM models, combined with industry-specific challenges, can lead to weak project planning, lack of accountability, lack of stakeholder engagement, lack of integration, shallow risk management, and lack of motivation, resulting in poor quality and loss of money and time. Consequently, various global INGOs have recognized these issues and acknowledged the role of PM in their practical policies, such as the Program Manual of Mercy Corps (2012). Golini et al. (2015) have empirically confirmed the role of PM models in improving performance in the industry (Dumrak et al. 2017), making them essential for the sustainability of reproductive health development projects.

Scholars have identified numerous limitations and challenges to the successful implementation of standard project management models within INGOs. Vahanvati and Mulligan (2017) determined three key impediments to using these models in post-disaster reconstruction projects: inflexibility, the tendency to address reconstruction as a technical pursuit, and focusing on outcomes rather than the process. However, a common theme in the literature is the connection between IDAPs and broader, long-term social goals (McEvoy et al. 2016; Vahanvati and Mulligan 2017; Steinfort 2017). Ika and Donnelly (2017) further categorized success criteria into PM conditions namely, design, leadership, monitoring, and stakeholder coordination; institutional conditions namely, beneficiary capacity and organizational capacity of implementing organizations; and structural conditions namely, contextual environment, accountability, and public participation).

Recent studies by Matos et al. (2019) have confirmed that the classical PM models are not suitable for use in the INGOs sector without adaptation. In response, PMI has funded several research studies and Ph.D. theses, including work by Steinfort (2010), which concluded that:

> It has become apparent that traditional project management methods, such as those addressed by the PMBOK, do not necessarily work well in these environments. Thus, a valuable topic of research for project management theory is uncovering the tacit assumptions regarding PM performance, namely the antecedents of PM best practice. (Steinfort 2010)

Therefore, this book introduces an adaptive and value-driven PM model designed to enhance the performance of IDAPs in order to better serve crisis-affected populations and vulnerable communities. It is widely recognized that this type of model should be implemented without delay.

References

Abd Elhameed AT (2018) Analyzing the project management body of knowledge (PMBOK) through theoretical lenses: a study to enhance the PMBOK through the project management theories. PM World Journal 6:1–31

AbouAssi K, & Makhlouf N (2018) A comparison of nonprofits' application of project management practices. J Muslim Philanthr & Civ Soc 2(2)

Accountable Now (2019) About accountable now. https://accountablenow.org/about-accountable-now/

Aldashev G, Navarra C (2018) Development NGOS: basic facts. Ann Public Coop Econ 89(1):125–155

Altayeb MM, Alhasanat MB (2014) Implementing total quality management (TQM) in the Palestinian construction industry. Int J Qual & Reliab Manag 31(8):878–887

Alves EJ, Gonçalves CA (2018) Project portfolio prioritization framework—case study applied at a Brazilian semiconductor subsidiary. Iberoam J Proj Manag 9(1):55–77

Anderson K, Lannon J (2018) Project management performance assessment in the non-profit sector. Proj Manag Res Pract 5:1–20

Baker B (2018) Project quality management practice and theory. Am J Manag 18(3):10–17

Boomsma R, O'Dwyer B (2019) Constituting the governable NGO: The correlation between conduct and counter-conduct in the evolution of funder-NGO accountability relations. Acc Organ Soc 72:1–20

Bouranta N, Psomas E, Suárez-Barraza MF, Jaca C (2019) The key factors of total quality management in the service sector: a cross-cultural study. Benchmarking: Int J 26(3):893–921

CARE International. (2017). She is a humanitarian: women's participation in humanitarian action drawing on global trends and evidence from Jordan and the Philippines. https://reliefweb.int/report/world/she-humanitarian-women-s-participation-humanitarian-action-drawing-global-trends-and

Crack AM (2018) The regulation of international NGOS: assessing the effectiveness of the INGO accountability charter. VOLUNTAS: Int J Volunt Nonprofit Organ 29(2):419–429

Core Humanitarian Standard (CHS) (2019) Core humanitarian standard on quality and accountability. https://corehumanitarianstandard.org/

Davis JM, Garb Y (2019) Participatory shaping of community futures in e-waste processing hubs: complexity. Conflict and stewarded convergence in a Palestinian context. Dev Policy Rev 37(1):67–89

Dumrak J, Baroudi B, Hadjinicolaou N (2017) Exploring the association between project management knowledge areas and sustainable outcomes. Procedia Engineering 182:157–164

Fox J (2018) The political construction of accountability keywords. In: Nelson E, Bloom G, & Shankland A. (eds) Accountability for health equity: galvanizing a movement for universal health coverage. IDS Bulletin 49.2. IDS, Brighton

Friedson E (2001) Professionalism: The Third Logic, Polity Press, Cambridge

Golini R, Landoni P (2014) International development projects by non-governmental organizations: An evaluation of the need for specific project management and appraisal tools. Impact Assessment and Project Appraisal 32(2):121–135

Golini R, Kalchschmidt M, Landoni P (2015) Adoption of project management practices: The impact on international development projects of non-governmental organizations. Int J Project Manage 33(3):650–663

Gomes CF, Small MH, Yasin MM (2019) Towards excellence in managing the public-sector project cycle: A TQM context. Int J Public Sect Manag 32(2):207–228

Hermano V, Martín-Cruz N (2019) Expanding the knowledge on project management standards: a look into the PMBOK® with dynamic lenses. In: Project Management and Engineering Research. Springer, Cham, pp 19–34

Hermano V, López-Paredes A, Martín-Cruz N, Pajares J (2013) How to manage international development (ID) projects successfully. Is the PMD pro guide going to the right direction? Int J Proj Manag 31(1):22–30

Hilhorst D (2015) Taking accountability to the next level. In on the road to Istanbul: How can the World Humanitarian Summit make humanitarian response more effective? CHS Alliance, 104–112

Hilhorst D, Desportes I, de Milliano CWJ (2019) Humanitarian governance and resilience building: Ethiopia in comparative perspective. Disasters 43(2):109–131

Howsawi E, Eager D, Bagia R, Niebecker K (2014) Project management during national crisis: concept development. Int Rev Manag Bus Res 3(1):412–422

Ika LA (2012) Project management for development in Africa: why projects are failing and what can be done about it. Proj Manag J 43(4):27–41

Ika LA, Donnelly J (2017) Success conditions for international development capacity building projects. Int J Project Manage 35(1):44–63

Ika LA, Hodgson D (2014) Learning from international development projects: blending critical project studies and critical development studies. Int J Project Manage 32(7):1182–1196

Ika LA, Saint-Macary J (2012) The project planning myth in international development. Int J Manag Proj Bus 5(3):420–439

Jamal A, Baldwin C (2019) Angels of mercy or smiling western invaders? community's perception of NGOs in northwest Pakistan. Int Soc Work 62(1):89–104

Karia N, Saleh FIM (2021) The effect of TQM practices on INGOs' staff work-related attitudes. Benchmarking: Int J 29(2):596–621

Keleckaite M, Meiliene E (2015) The importance of project management methodologies and tools in non-governmental organizations: case study of Lithuania and Germany. PM World Journal 4(7):1–17

Koskela L, Howell G (2002) The theory of project management: explanation to novel methods. In Proceedings IGLC 10(1):1–11

Kwak YH, Anbari FT (2009) Analyzing project management research: Perspectives from top management journals. Int J Project Manage 27(5):435–446

Lacruz A, Cunha E (2018) Project management office in non-governmental organizations: an ex post facto study. Revista De Gestão 25(2):212–227

Lassa JA (2019) Roles of non-government organizations in disaster risk reduction. Oxford Research Encyclopedia of Natural Hazard Science

Levie F, Burke CM, Lannon J (2017) Filling the gaps: an investigation of project governance in a non-governmental organisation's response to the Haiti earthquake disaster. Int J Project Manage 35(5):875–888

Lousberg LHMJ (2006) Towards a theory of project management. In: 3rd intern. SCRI Symposium. University of Salford, pp 40–51

Mahmoud AB, Alatrash M, Fuxman L, Hack-Polay D, Grigoriou N (2019) Validating a new total quality management-benchmarking measurement model in an international humanitarian setting. Nonprofit Manag Leadersh 30(1):167–182

Matos PV, Romão M, Sarmento JM, Abaladas A (2019) The adoption of project management methodologies and tools by NGDOs: a mixed methods perspective. J Bus Res 101:651–659

McEvoy P, Brady M, Munck R (2016) Capacity development through international projects: a complex adaptive systems perspective. Int J Manag Proj Bus 9(3):528–545

Mercy Corps (2012) Program management manual. https://www.mercycorps.org/sites/default/files/programmanagementmanualpmm.pdf

Nanthagopan Y, Williams N, Thompson K (2019) Levels and interconnections of project success in development projects by non-governmental organizations (NGOs). Int J Manag Proj Bus 12(2):487–511

Omar MFHM, Ismail SHS (2019) Development of NGO Governance in Malaysia: Lessons from Indonesia and Jordan. Al-Qanatir: Int J Islamic Stud 13(2):70–80

Opdyke A, Javernick-Will A, Koschmann M (2018) A comparative analysis of coordination, participation, and training in post-disaster shelter projects. Sustainability 10(11):4241

Penn H (2019) Patronage, welfare, tenders, private consultancies and expert measurement: what is happening in early childhood education and care. In: Early childhood and development work. Palgrave Macmillan, pp 1–15

Pollack J (2007) The changing paradigms of project management. Int J Project Manage 25(3):266–274

Project Management Institute (PMI) (2017) Project management body of knowledge (PMBOK® Guide). Project Management Institute Inc., PA

Rahman HA (2018) Community based approach towards disaster management in Malaysia (Pendekatan berasaskan komuniti dalam pengurusan bencana di Malaysia). Asian J Environ, Hist Herit 2(2)

Rani SS (2018) The application of total quality management (TQM in not for profit organizations (NPOs)—with special reference to The Akshaya Patra Foundation in India. DHARANA—Bhavan's Int J Bus 11(2):42–56

Rehacek P (2017) Application and usage of the standards for project management and their comparison. J Eng Appl Sci 12(4):994–1002

Robehmed S (2019) Designing user-centered humanitarian technologies with displaced people in Iraq: lessons from Refunite's mobile family tracing platform. Int Migr 57(2):109–120

Rohaizan R, Tan PY (2011) The practices of TQM among MS: ISO 9000 certified company. In: 3rd international conference on information and financial engineering IPEDR, p 12

Saleh FIM, Sweis RJ, Abdelqader BY, Abdallah AB, & Arafeh M (2017) The Effect of TQM Dimensions on the Performance of International Non-Governmental Organisations Operating in Jordan. Int J Prod and Qual Manag 21(4):443–459
Salah S, Rahim A (2019) Six sigma and TQM. An integrated company-wide management system. Springer, Cham, pp 39–47
Saleh FIM, Karia N (2020) Management for international development and aid projects: A new conceptual model. Nonprofit Manag Leadersh 31(2):373–386
Sanderson D (2017) Collaboration and cross-sector coordination for humanitarian assistance in a disaster recovery setting. Oxford Research Encyclopedia of Natural Hazard Science.
Shaw R (2016) Community-based disaster risk reduction. Oxford Research Encyclopedia of Natural Hazard Science
Sphere Project (2019a) The sphere project in brief. http://www.sphereproject.org/about/
Sphere Project (2019b) Core humanitarian standards (CHS). https://www.spherestandards.org/humanitarian-standards/core-humanitarian-standard/
Steinfort P (2010) Understanding the antecedents of project management best practice—lessons to be learned for and from aid/relief projects. Dissertation. https://researchbank.rmit.edu.au/eserv/rmit:7526/Steinfort.pdf
Steinfort P, Walker DH (2007) Critical success factors in project management globally and how they may be applied to aid projects. In: PMOZ achieving excellence-4th annual project management Australia conference. Inovoke.
Steinfort P, Walker DH (2008) A critique of the PMI post-disaster rebuild methodology. In Proceedings of PMI Research Conference
Steinfort P (2017) Community and post-disaster program management methodology. Int J Project Manage 35(5):788–801
Sweis RJ, Saleh FIM, Dahiyat SE, Sweis NJ, Saleh RA, & Diab H (2016) Benchmarking of TQM practices in INGOs: a literature review. Benchmarking: Int J 23(1):236–261
Vahanvati M, Mulligan M (2017) A new model for effective post-disaster housing reconstruction: Lessons from Gujarat and Bihar in India. Int J Project Manage 35(5):802–817
Van Kemenade E, Hardjono TW (2019) Twenty-first century total quality management: the emergence paradigm. TQM J 31(2):150–166
Yamin M, Sim AKS (2016) Critical success factors for international development projects in Maldives. Int J Manag Proj Bus 9(3):481–504
Yao YAO (2016) The rational and behavioral view in project management. DEStech Transactions on Social Science, Education and Human Science (ICSS). https://www.dpi-proceedings.com/index.php/dtssehs/article/view/9105
Yasmin S, Ghafran C (2019) The problematics of accountability: internal responses to external pressures in exposed organizations. Critical Perspectives on Accounting.

Chapter 3
Complexities of International Development and Aid Projects

3.1 Introduction

Project complexity has been widely discussed in the PM literature (Yugue and Maximiano 2012) as a key factor in project failure (Qazi et al. 2016). It is therefore essential to measure it proactively to ensure project success. IDAPs are no exception. Moreover, the foreign context of IDAPs makes them high-risk projects (Dandage et al. 2018). Those implemented by INGOs are especially complex on a socio-political scale, as Ika and Hodgson (2014) observed.

Generally, the source of project complexity can be internal or external to the project or organization carrying it out. Internal complexity can be generated by human and system behavior as well as uncertainty (PMI 2017). On the other hand, external complexity can come from tangible and intangible environmental factors, such as intended social changes in targeted communities (Bayiley and Teklu 2016), socio-political aspects (Matos et al. 2019), and the location or work setting of the INGO project (Moroto et al. 2018). Therefore, Tang (2019) stated that the goal of "Poverty Reduction" is enough to distinguish IDAPs from projects in the private sector, which are relatively simpler and involve basic customer–seller equations rather than complex and multi-level stakeholder management and accountability.

This book seeks to tackle the complexities of IDAPs via their proposed domains and processes. To this end, the present chapter begins by exploring the possible challenges associated with such projects.

3.2 Dimensions of IDAPs Complexity

Despite the positive ambitions and goals of IDAPs, they are often under pressure from their donors to comply with the policies of their originating countries. This pressure can create a conflict of interest between their mission and social goals, related political

F. I. Mahmoud Saleh and N. Karia, *Value-driven Management for International Development and Aid Projects*, https://doi.org/10.1007/978-981-97-3666-9_3

aims and agendas, and potential benefits. Bayiley and Teklu (2016) suggest that this pressure adds complexity to the projects within this sector. Nevertheless, citizens prefer IDAPs to governmental projects when trust is an issue with their governments or when gaps in needs still need to be filled (Jackman 2018). This presents further challenges and threats to the success, performance, and sustainability of projects in view of the realities and contextual aspects on the ground.

The IDAPs face numerous challenges, which include, but are not limited to, political (Wildeman 2017), legislative and logistic (Tirmizi and Vogelsang 2016), and ethical concerns (Jackman 2018). Furthermore, there is a risk of violent incidents or even terrorism (Lambert 2018), and stakeholders may express doubts about the relevance and efficacy of the aid provided (Ubalijoro 2018) and the legitimacy of the services rendered (Noh 2018). Additionally, there are issues such as a lack of local capacities (McEvoy et al. 2016), language barriers (Mancuso Brehm 2019), ethnic conflicts (Bayiley and Teklu 2016), and the authoritarian nature of some governments (Harms 2017).

Haapala and Keskinen (2018) have identified four tensions between the directive policies at the top of IDAPs and the domestic realities and, in turn, project implementation. These tensions are: (1) international donor policy; (2) national recipient policies; (3) two-directional pressure (up and down); and (4) the tension that results from the mismatch between the project design and local realities. As a result, IDAPs activities are often at odds with social norms (Haapala and Keskinen 2018), religion (Ismail 2018), or cultural values in the targeted areas (Dandage et al. 2018). Smith (2018) further suggests that the insensitivity to ethnic conflicts in the regions where INGOs operate often exacerbates disputes. Howsawi et al. (2014) conclude that PM during national crises may be impacted by five factors: urgency, government interventions, emerging threats and opportunities, resource and supply disturbance, and uncertainty.

The international financing of IDAPs cannot be separated from international conflict and the political goals of donor countries. The dynamics of international development and the covert competition between international players to extend their influence to developing countries play a key role in forming the objectives of global aid and development projects. In most cases, dedicated budgets for international development are created to serve political aims or intentional social changes in the targeted countries. This results in a lack of attention to the actual needs and priorities on the ground, reliance on irrelevant theories of change or technical standards, and, most importantly, allocating the majority of funds to objectives that are not relevant to the targeted people. For instance, each USAID country mission must include USAID's global indicators, the mission's indicators side by side with the specific indicators for each IDAP.

McEwan (2009) and Ziai (2011) challenge the notion that development is a modern phenomenon driven by the decisions of Western experts, arguing that its meaning is different in various contexts and times. They have argued that development is a "dominant, universalizing, and arrogant" discourse of the North, which is based on European cultures and reflective of a Western worldview. This implies a standardized diagnosis of social issues, with a failure to take into account the constantly changing cultures of those affected by development policies. Consequently, development can be seen as destructive and damaging to the lives of the subaltern if the gap between global standards and the local realities and leadership is not bridged.

The complexity of managing IDAPs arises from the social and humanitarian objectives of such projects, as well as the diversity of stakeholders (Latif and Williams 2017). This complexity is further compounded by the need for effective project communication and stakeholder engagement for project success (Nguyen et al. 2018). Core Humanitarian Standards (CHS 2014) emphasize the importance of participation and inclusion for IDAPs; however, these are simultaneously seen as sources of complexity by literature and practitioners alike (Chouinard and Milley 2018; Davis and Garb 2019). Defining the target communities of IDAPs is a complex task, involving numerous factors such as religion, caste, tribal and ethnic groups, associations, and language (Chouinard and Milley 2018).

The literature on IDAPs has widely discussed the factors of risk and uncertainty. The sector has grown increasingly unpredictable due to competition and a lack of funding (Zhu et al. 2018). For instance, implementers of IDAPs are often not aware of the timeframes for responding to displacement crises, leaving them in a precarious position of potential funding discontinuity. Suggestion: This has been proven by the succession of refugee crises in Syria, Yemen, and Ukraine, each of which has resulted in adjustments to the previous crisis's donor priorities. Furthermore, responding to the negative consequences of displacement involves particular complexities linked to socio-political negotiations with refugees and host communities (Oliver-Smith 2019). In this context, Cantekin (2019) identified eight pre-migration themes of experience that refugees might face, including arrest and abuses of human rights, armed conflicts, lack of basic physical needs, body injury, witnessing violence against others, family-related fears, sectarian discrimination, and loss of relatives. He also classified the difficulties that refugees might encounter post-migration under eight themes: family loss and separation, loss of identity and civic documentation, gender-based issues, coping difficulties, livelihood challenges, the situation in sending countries, health issues, and living conditions at the camps. Consequently, the complexity factors faced by IDAPs implementers can be summarized as follows (See Table 3.1).

Coordination and complementation are additional sources of complexity that are unique to this industry. To further explore this notion, we will delve into the specifics in the following section.

3.3 Coordination and Complementation Versus Competition

Competition between INGOs is connected to the shifting flow of funds (Martinez and Cooper 2017) and the limited amount of money available in comparison to the growing poverty, needs, and number of vulnerable people (Egger 2018; Laguna-Salvadó et al. 2018). This decreased funding could lead to tension or alliances among

Table 3.1 The complexity factors of IDAPs

	Complexity factor	References
1.	The complexity of donor's policies, regulations, and agendas	Wildeman (2017), Haapala and Keskinen (2018), Shams (2017), Martinez and Cooper (2017), Szalai (2018), Kloster (2019)
2.	Sensitivity of local cultures and differences	Bayiley and Teklu (2016), Haapala and Keskinen (2018), Mati (2017), Ismail (2018), Dandage et al. (2018), Smith (2018), Chouinard and Milley (2018)
3.	Uncertainty and risky environment of business	Howsawi et al. (2014), Howe and Stites (2018), Zhu et al. (2018), Larson and Foropon (2018)
4.	Local capacities	Howe and Stites (2018), McEvoy et al. (2016), Adem et al. (2018), Haapala and Keskinen (2018)
5.	The complexity of needs and expectations, nature of interventions, and relevance of implemented activities	Dahi (2014), Levie et al. (2017), Ubalijoro (2018), Noh (2018), Haapala and Keskinen (2018), Tang (2019), Bayiley and Teklu (2016)
6.	The complexity of working with local governments and regulations	Anderson (2018), Harms (2017), Smith (2018), Sida et al. (2016), Carpi and Pınar Şenoğuz (2018)
7.	The complexity of work setting and safety and security	Nemeth and Mauslein (2017), Schneiker (2018), Lambert (2018), Moroto et al. (2018)
8.	The complexity of industry-specificities	CHS (2014), Davis and Garb (2019), Chouinard and Milley (2018)
9.	Diversity of stakeholders	Levie et al. (2017), Latif and Williams (2017), Larson and Foropon (2018), Nguyen et al. (2018), Chouinard and Milley (2018), Elbanna et al. (2019)

INGOs, as well as the race to be present in affected areas, even competing with local NGOs (Martinez and Cooper 2017). This could mean that INGOs lose the assumed positive heterogeneous nature they should possess (Davis 2019); however, competition also has the potential to encourage managerial boundaries and improve INGO performance (Laguna-Salvadó et al. 2018). Ahmed and Abdullahi (2017) have argued that IDAPs implementers must strive to be better in order to compete with existing organizations and with new organizations that are quickly cropping up.

Recent discourse has suggested that there are numerous benefits to donors providing direct funding to local NGOs, which has created tension between INGOs and local NGOs. Despite this, most donors prefer to have one contract with a more established partner, thus avoiding the hassle of managing multiple contracts (Ismail 2019) and transferring potential risks associated with working with less mature local parties to the INGOs (Majid et al. 2018).

Competition among INGOs for contracts can cause a diminishment in development efforts (Smith 2018). This has a detrimental effect on vulnerable people. In their attempts to secure funds, INGOs often opt for the easier, shorter routes of targeting and programming rather than exploring deeper to identify and address entrenched needs, complex vulnerabilities, and challenging contexts (Davis 2019). This reduces the relevance, effectiveness, and sustainability of the IDAPs. Moreover, INGOs are beginning to adjust their strategies to align with the interests and preferences of donors (Kloster 2019) rather than adhering to the people-centered strategies and IDAPs advocated by the Core Humanitarian Standard (CHS 2014).

Inadequate emergency responses and poor coordination are not uncommon in crises (Levie et al. 2017). However, INGOs must coordinate with each other rather than compete (Smith 2018). This requires them to put aside any competition they may have with one another, as they are unable to work alone. For example, the delivery of services and assistance must be done in line with the government's policies (Anderson 2018) and should be coordinated with Inter-Governmental Organizations (Johnson 2016). Failing to consider the role of the government when providing services to the community can result in the high or full dependency of vulnerable people on INGOs, which can ultimately lead to the failure of the SDGs of IDAPs (Smith 2018). On the other hand, weak governmental structures in the targeted areas and control or even conflict over resources can create a fragile environment for IDAP implementers to easily gain a foothold in the country (Szalai 2018). This is not the case for all countries, such as Turkey and Jordan, which are both refugee-hosting countries. For instance, the United Nations Office for the Coordination of Humanitarian Affairs (OCHA) took two years to establish its presence in Turkey (Sida et al. 2016). Moreover, INGOs must partner with a national organization in order to implement IDAPs in Turkey (Carpi and Pınar Şenoğuz 2018). In Jordan, each INGO must be registered with the Ministry of Social Development and each IDAP must be approved by the Ministry of Planning and International Cooperation (MoPIC) (Johnson 2016).

Coordination is an essential element of the industry, as established by CHS (2014), and can be described as a systematic set of measures that aim to protect vulnerable individuals (Begum and Mome 2019). However, the implementation of coordination can be complex, with Oliver-Smith (2019) noting several challenges, including who should lead and how; the capacity and roles of the host government; the governance structure of organizations; power dynamics; the balance between partnership and results-oriented approaches; and issues of accountability.

In 2016, the World Humanitarian Summit culminated in the signing of the "Grand Bargain" Agreement. This agreement outlined ten goals to be pursued by international donors and the humanitarian community, with a particular focus on improving coordination, reducing duplication, harmonizing reporting, and promoting engagement between humanitarian and development organizations (Dijkzeul and Sandvik 2019; Hallwright and Handmer 2019; Hilhorst et al. 2019). In addition, joint assessments and participation were also to be increased.

Box 2.1 Coordination in the Syrian Refugee Crisis

UNHCR is the central coordination body among all INGOs in the Syrian refugee response. To support this, they have adopted the cluster approach, which brings INGOs and other actors together under sectorial platforms or coordination working groups on both country and regional levels. These working groups include the protection sector, education sector, livelihoods sector, health sector, durable solutions, basic needs, gender-based violence, and more. UNHCR's sector coordination system provides figures of affected people, monthly reporting of those reached, who is doing what, financial tracking of the funds, and management of coordinated needs assessments (UNHCR 2019c). Cross-sectoral coordination is also operationalized through the inter-sector working group hosted by UNHCR. Both among and inter-sector coordination are essential in such contexts, as Sanderson (2017) advocates.

It can be concluded that INGOs should improve the performance of their IDAPs in order to enhance their competitiveness when acquiring funds and targeting people of a certain quality. This would also help to facilitate and sustain the outcomes of these IDAPs. Furthermore, they should work to improve performance and introduce coordination functions in order to take advantage of coordination opportunities and avoid any potential negative impacts or missed opportunities due to a lack of coordination.

References

Adem SA, Childerhouse P, Egbelakin T, Wang B (2018) International and local NGO supply chain collaboration. Journal of Humanitarian Logistics and Supply Chain Management. https://doi.org/10.1108/jhlscm-05-2017-0020

Ahmed S, Abdullahi AM (2017) Leadership and project success in development sector. Journal of Economics and Management 30:5–19

Anderson JL (2018) Global humanitarian organizations and African goals: The case of Médecins Sans Frontières in South Africa. Afr Foreign Policies Int Inst:229–244. https://doi.org/10.1057/978-1-137-57574-6_15

Bayiley YT, Teklu GK (2016) Success factors and criteria in the management of international development projects. Int J Manag Proj Bus 9(3):562–582. https://doi.org/10.1108/ijmpb-06-2015-0046

Begum MM, Momen MN (2019) Coordination does matter for disaster management in Bangladesh. In: Disaster risk reduction. Palgrave Macmillan, Singapore, pp 19–35

Cantekin D (2019) Syrian refugees living on the edge: policy and practice implications for mental health and psychosocial wellbeing. Int Migr 57(2):200–220

Carpi E, Pınar Şenoğuz H (2018) Refugee hospitality in Lebanon and Turkey. On making "the other." Int Mig. https://doi.org/10.1111/imig.12471.

Chouinard JA, Milley P (2018) Uncovering the mysteries of inclusion: empirical and methodological possibilities in participatory evaluation in an international context. Eval Program Plann 67:70–78

Dahi O (2014) The refugee crisis in Lebanon and Jordan: the need for economic development spending, The Syria crisis, displacement and protection, FMR 47, pp 11–13

Dandage R, Mantha SS, Rane SB (2018) Ranking the risk categories in international projects using the TOPSIS method. Int J Manag Proj Bus 11(2):317–331

Davis JM (2019) Real "non-governmental" aid and poverty: comparing privately and publicly financed NGOs in Canada. Can J Dev Stud/Revue canadienne d'études du développement:1–18

Davis JM, Garb Y (2019) Participatory shaping of community futures in e-waste processing hubs: complexity, conflict and stewarded convergence in a Palestinian context. Development Policy Review 37(1):67–89

Dijkzeul D, Sandvik KB (2019) A world in turmoil: governing risk, establishing order in humanitarian crises. Disasters.

Egger C (2018) Just part-time lovers? Competition, coercive coordination, and friendship among international INGOs. Camb Rev Int Aff 30(4):394–414. https://doi.org/10.1080/09557571.2017.1422481

Elbanna A, Bunker D, Levine L, Sleigh A (2019) Emergency management in the changing world of social media: Framing the research agenda with the stakeholders through engaged scholarship. Int J Inf Manag 47:112–120. https://doi.org/10.1016/j.ijinfomgt.2019.01.011

Haapala J, Keskinen M (2018) Influence of different discourses on the outcomes of development policies and projects: Insights from water project implementation in Nepal. Environ Policy Gov 28(3):141–152

Hallwright J, Handmer J (2019) Accountability and transparency in disaster aid: cyclone pam in Vanuatu. Int J Disaster Risk Reduct, 101104

Harms H (2017) Challenges for sustainable development of informal settlements and of desert new towns in Cairo. In: Revitalizing city districts. Springer, Cham, pp 147–169

Hilhorst D, Desportes I, de Milliano CWJ (2019) Humanitarian governance and resilience building: Ethiopia in comparative perspective. Disasters 43(S2):S109–S131. https://doi.org/10.1111/disa.12332

Howe K, Stites E (2018) Partners under pressure: humanitarian action for the Syria crisis. Disasters. https://doi.org/10.1111/disa.12298

Howsawi E, Eager D, Bagia R, Niebecker K (2014) Project management during national crisis: concept development. Int Rev Manag Bus Res 3(1):412–422

Ika LA, Hodgson D (2014) Learning from international development projects: Blending critical project studies and critical development studies. Int J Project Manag 32(7):1182–1196. https://doi.org/10.1016/j.ijproman.2014.01.004

Ismail Z (2018) Using zakat for international development. University of Birmingham. Retrieved from: https://opendocs.ids.ac.uk/opendocs/handle/123456789/13647

Jackman M (2018) Reaching out: navigating the ethical, legislative, and physical obstacles to providing assistance to migrants in Morocco.

Johnson T (2016) Cooperation, co-optation, competition, conflict: international bureaucracies and non-governmental organizations in an interdependent world. Rev Int Polit Econ 23(5):737–767. https://doi.org/10.1080/09692290.2016.1217902

Kloster MO (2019) Why it hurts–save the children Norway and the dilemmas of 'going global'. In: Forum for development studies, vol. 46, no. 1. Routledge, pp 109–130

Laguna-Salvadó L, Lauras M, Okongwu U, Comes T (2018) A multicriteria master planning DSS for a sustainable humanitarian supply chain. Ann Oper Res. https://doi.org/10.1007/s10479-018-2882-3

Lambert KM (2018) Assessing the impact of the political environment on INGO vulnerability to terrorist attack. Risk Hazards Cris Public Policy 9(4):431–454

Larson PD, Foropon C (2018) Process improvement in humanitarian operations: an organisational theory perspective. Int J Prod Res 56(21):6828–6841

Latif KF, Williams N (2017) Team effectiveness in non-governmental organizations (NGOs) projects. Eval Program Plann 64:20–32. https://doi.org/10.1016/j.evalprogplan.2017.05.004

Majid N, Abdirahman K, Poole L, Willitts-King B (2018) Funding to local humanitarian actors Somalia case study, HPG working paper. Overseas Development Institute. Retrieved from https://www.odi.org/publications/11212-funding-local-humanitarian-actors-somalia-case-study

Martinez DE, Cooper DJ (2017) Assembling international development: accountability and the disarticulation of a social movement. Acc Organ Soc 63:6–20. https://doi.org/10.1016/j.aos.2017.02.002

Mati JM (2017) Philanthropy in contemporary Africa: a review. Volunt Rev 1(6):1–100. https://doi.org/10.1163/24054933-12340014

Matos PV, Romão M, Sarmento JM, Abaladas A (2019) The adoption of project management methodologies and tools by NGDOs: a mixed methods perspective. J Bus Res. https://doi.org/10.1016/j.jbusres.2019.01.067

McEvoy P, Brady M, Munck R (2016) Capacity development through international projects: a complex adaptive systems perspective. Int J Manag Proj Bus 9(3):528–545. https://doi.org/10.1108/ijmpb-08-2015-0072

McEwan C (2009) Postcolonialism and development. Routledge, New York

Moroto H, Sakamoto M, Ahmed T (2018) Possible factors influencing NGOs' project locations for disaster management in Bangladesh. Int J Disaster Risk Reduc 27:248–264. https://doi.org/10.1016/j.ijdrr.2017.10.011

Ndlovu-Gatsheni S (2013) Coloniality of power in postcolonial Africa: myths of decolonization. J Retracing Afr 3(1):96–98

Nemeth SC, Mauslein JA (2017) Generosity is a dangerous game: aid allocation and the risks of terrorism. Terror Polit Violence:1–19. https://doi.org/10.1080/09546553.2017.1377074

Nguyen TS, Mohamed S, Panuwatwanich K (2018) Stakeholder management in complex project: review of contemporary literature. J Eng Proj Prod Manag 8(2)

Noh J-E (2018) The legitimacy of development nongovernmental organizations as global citizenship education providers in Korea. Educ Citizsh Soc Justice 174619791879997. https://doi.org/10.1177/1746197918799972

Oliver-Smith A (2019) Disasters and large-scale population dislocations: international and national responses. Oxford Research Encyclopedia of Natural Hazard Science, https://doi.org/10.1093/acrefore/9780199389407.013.224

Project Management Institute (2017) Project management body of knowledge (PMBOK Guide ®). Project Management Institute Inc., PA

Qazi A, Quigley J, Dickson A, Kirytopoulos K (2016) Project complexity and risk management (ProCRiM): towards modelling project complexity driven risk paths in construction projects. Int J Project Manag 34(7):1183–1198

Schneiker A (2018) Risk-aware or risk-averse? Challenges in implementing security risk management within humanitarian NGOs. Risk, Hazards Cris Public Policy 9(2):107–131. https://doi.org/10.1002/rhc3.12136

Shams F (2017) Aid effectiveness in education: a case study of Pakistan from 2005–2015. Doctoral thesis, UCL (University College London).

Sida L, Trombetta L, Panero V (2016) Evaluation of OCHA response to the Syria crisis. UN-OCHA, March, 15.

Smith SR (2018) The future of nonprofit human services. Nonprofit Policy Forum 8(4):369–389. https://doi.org/10.1515/npf-2017-0019

Sphere Project (2019) Core humanitarian standards (CHS), https://www.spherestandards.org/humanitarian-standards/core-humanitarian-standard/

Szalai M (2018) "The international NGO triangle in the Mena region", MENARA working papers, Middle East and North Africa regional architecture: mapping geopolitical shifts, regional order and domestic transformations, retrieved from https://www.iai.it/sites/default/files/menara_wp_19.pdf

Tang L (2019) Mechanism innovation for poverty alleviation and development and precise poverty alleviation. In: The evolution of China's poverty alleviation and development policy (2001–2015). Springer, Singapore, pp 107–135

Tirmizi SA, Vogelsang JD (eds) (2016) Leading and managing in the social sector: strategies for advancing human dignity and social justice. Springer

Ubalijoro É (2018) Transforming community through feminine leadership. In: Leadership and power in international development: navigating the intersections of gender, culture, context, and sustainability. Emerald Publishing Limited, pp 83–97

Wildeman J (2017) Undermining the democratic process: The Canadian government suppression of Palestinian development aid projects. The Canadian Journal for Middle East Studies 2(1):2033

Zhu J, Ye S, Liu Y (2018) Legitimacy, board involvement, and resource competitiveness: drivers of NGO revenue diversification. Voluntas. https://doi.org/10.1007/s11266-018-0044-5
Ziai A (2011) Beyond post-development: Postcolonial perspectives on 'development.' Dev Chang 42(5):1297–1306

Chapter 4
Strategic Alignment and Management for IDAPs

4.1 Introduction

In Chapter 2, we explored the importance of taking into account the wider structural and contextual elements relating to IDAPs as part of the new required paradigm. Here, we go into greater detail about the specific and strategic links that must be considered when designing, planning, and executing IDAPs to start building blocks of this paradigm.

The essence of IDAPs should be to serve the interests of people of concern. However, in practice, this is rarely the case due to the dynamics of international development and how IDAPs are strategized and implemented. According to one of the former leaders of major international development programs in Jordan interviewed for this book, only 30% of the total budget of the program reaches the target program participants. Additionally, 10% of the indirect costs contribute to the in-country economy, but most of the major procurements are usually sourced from the donor's home country. Furthermore, the salaries of the project staff at the headquarters of the implementing organizations are also sourced from the donor's home country. This has led to accusations that international donors are flooding the market in the targeted countries with non-value-added funds and gaining political returns from the targeted countries without providing actual benefits.

The generous amount of international aid given to developing countries does not appear to be achieving the desired results. This chapter of the book, therefore, investigates ways to more effectively link projects to the various strategic dimensions. It aims to demonstrate how this alignment can be beneficial and not necessarily detrimental. The following sections of this chapter focus on the effective operationalization of alignment with a country's strategic plans and development goals, implementing organizations' strategies, global objectives of headquarters, and donor mandates in the design and implementation phases of IDAPs. Chapters 5 and 6 will delve further into the alignment with the most critical dimension, the priorities of

F. I. Mahmoud Saleh and N. Karia, *Value-driven Management for International Development and Aid Projects*, https://doi.org/10.1007/978-981-97-3666-9_4

Fig. 4.1 The process of IDAPs strategic alignment

those in need. Furthermore, this chapter concludes with how to track the achievement of these strategies to ensure ultimate accountability.

Therefore, this chapter provides practical strategies, tools, and insights to ensure the strategic alignment of IDAPs from the concept or design stages of the project through planning and implementation. Additionally, the last section offers guidance on how these alignments should be managed and monitored, as illustrated in Fig. 4.1.

4.2 Alignment with the Strategic Plans and Development Priorities of the Targeted Country

Aiming to coordinate and rationalize in-country development efforts and responses to man-made and natural disasters, if they occur, each country has its own development priorities and long-term strategies for development and disaster management. Generally speaking, these strategies, particularly in developing countries, are developed in line with the agreed-upon global development goals.

The most important global development goals are the Millennium Development Goals (MDGs) and the Sustainable Development Goals (SDGs). However, these two global goals differ in purpose, conception, and the political process driving their elaboration. The MDGs were a North–South aid agenda mostly relevant to developing countries and were crafted by development ministers and heads of development agencies. In contrast, the SDGs are a global agenda for sustainable development, setting targets for all countries, and emerged from the 2012 Rio+20 Conference, driven by environment ministers from countries in both the North and South. The MDGs focused on poverty alleviation, while the SDGs encompass ending poverty as a core objective as well as environmental, social, and economic sustainability. In terms of the process of drafting, the MDGs were formulated by a limited number of UN staff with limited input from other sources, while the SDGs are the result of two parallel processes combined to create a declaration at the 2015 General Assembly (Fukuda-Parr 2016).

Regardless of which global goals the developing countries are aligned with, the alignment of IDAPs with the strategic plans of the countries of concern has been widely acknowledged as a key success factor in the international development arena toward the ultimate sustainability of these projects (Bayiley and Teklu 2016).

Usually, the evaluation criteria for donor calls and funds for IDAPs include the criterion of alignment with SDGs and in-country development priorities, strategies, and crisis or disaster response plans. However, these intentions are often ignored or not fully operationalized when it comes to planning and implementing IDAPs on the ground, which is considered a major complexity factor for IDAPs. Therefore, the rest of this section provides specific processes on how to put these intentions into practice (Saleh and Karia 2020, 2022).

The strategic alignment and rationalization of IDAPs begin at the proposal stage. Consequently, the implementing organizations must demonstrate how their interventions will meet the specific objectives of the in-country plans. This should be done as part of the problem analysis section of the proposals. Explicit indicators should be included; for instance, humanitarian response projects should demonstrate how their proposed interventions are linked to development and peacebuilding, how the resilience of targeted people will be enhanced, and how the indirectly affected people, such as the hosting communities and other vulnerable people in the refugee crises, will not be ignored. The failure of INGOs to show this nexus and how the humanitarian proposal is connected is a common reason for rejection of the proposal. Suggestion: As a result, governmental collaboration and even permission for IDAPs will be impossible to achieve without strong evidence of how donors and implementing agencies would benefit citizens and infrastructure, both of which are likely to be impacted by emerging crises.

The same applies to the IDAPs that target the development priorities of developing countries. Before submitting their development proposals, the implementing organizations should be ready with explicit evidence of their relevancy and contribution to in-country development problems and poverty. Such as unemployment rates, the livelihoods of poor people, gender inequality, water scarcity, and environmental problems.

The specific considerations for humanitarian and development proposals, concepts, or business cases include, but are not limited to:

- To what country-level, regional-level, or inter-agency humanitarian response does the proposal contribute?
- The sectors targeted by the proposed interventions.
- The total number of affected people, and the proportion of them that the proposed intervention will reach.
- How the needs of vulnerable citizens will be addressed along with the needs of directly affected people is particularly important in refugee-related and man-made crises.
- The preliminary consultations are done by the implementing organizations with the relevant governmental agencies before developing the planned interventions
- The expected contribution of proposed interventions to the resilience of the country and its ability to respond to similar future crises or disasters.

- The graduation, resilience, nexus, and sustainability pathways of the interventions needed for sustaining interventions to substitute the supposed temporary presence and departure of the implementing organization. This might include showing the clear, durable solution pathways that will be secured. Such as enhancing the readiness of targeted people for integration into the refugee-hosting country, voluntary return, or restatement to a third country if applicable.
- Provide critical revision and, in turn, an understanding of the key development priorities and concerns of the targeted country.
- Provide the explicitly expected contributions of the proposed interventions to the key identified in-country development problems.
- Provide a fair analysis of the conflict sensitivity considerations to avoid any negative or unintended effects on in-country peacebuilding or political conflicts.

4.3 Alignment with the Strategic Objectives of the Implementing Organization

A key player and implementer of IDAPs in crisis-affected regions and developing countries are INGOs. These organizations often operate according to organizational strategies and business plans. The strategic alignment of IDAPs with the strategies of the implementing organizations is a criterion for mature INGOs to determine whether or not to pursue funding opportunities. This is also a criterion for donors who want to know how their funds are being used to serve the strategies of the implementing organizations, and these organizations are not just seeking funds to achieve their financial portfolio targets.

When calls for proposals are raised, the senior management of in-country missions should conduct a GO/NGO exercise to determine whether to pursue the financing opportunity. Usually, this exercise entails an assessment of the following aspects:

- The fitness of the proposal for the strategic priorities of the in-country mission.
- The ability to scale proposed activities.
- The ability to leverage the in-country global experience of implementing INGO and the ability to incorporate learning agendas.
- Financial impact of the bid and the positive impact on the financial health of the in-country mission.
- The availability of comprehensive risk assessment and mitigation strategies.
- The probability of success and the donor's perception of the INGO in terms of its competitiveness, reputation, and past experience, as well as the absence of pre-orientation of bis to a particular company or contractor.
- The ability to produce a high-quality proposal in the allotted timeframe or the preparation for the proposal in advance of the solicitation being released.
- The capacity to successfully implement the scope of work, adherence to internal and external technical excellence, and the availability of systems for quality implementation.

Typically, the GO/NOGO process concentrates on the capability of the in-country mission to pursue the funding opportunities, the likelihood of success in securing and executing these possibilities, as well as the technical and financial returns.

In certain circumstances, in-country missions may implement global-level and headquarters strategies without modification. However, this is not the reality for several large INGOs, such as CARE International and Mercy Corps, whose country offices must devise strategies that are consistent with the confederation strategy. In these cases, the GO/NOGO processes will not be sufficient to ensure strategic alignment, particularly for those INGOs that have centralized global strategic tracking platforms or performance systems. Consequently, the GO/NOGO processes should be supplemented with additional strategic alignment exercises that can take the form of checklists or program quality markers.

In addition to the GO/NOGO questions, the complementary aspects that should be considered in the design phases of the IDAPs are mostly related to program quality concerns. Therefore, it is critical to ensure that the projects are developed not just in accordance with global-level strategies and headquarters but also to ensure that the programs are designed at the required levels of quality, depending on the quality measures of the organizations. These aspects may include but are not limited to, (Sweis et al. 2016; Saleh and Karia 2022):

- **Alignment with the global-level strategies and technical guidelines**: this might include a requirement to use a minimum number of indicators and use specific technical standards.
- **Accountability to effective populations**: the proposals should outline how the community feedback mechanisms are included and resourced for lifting the voice of targeted people and program participants.
- **Do no harm**: at least, the proposals should include specific measures for mitigating the risks of safeguarding, sexual abuse and exploitation, misuse of power, and fraud.
- **Partnerships, collaboration, and coordination**: the proposals should show how partnerships and coordination with the relevant local actors will be undertaken, including how the objectives of proposed actions fit into the strategic plans of all partners or consortium members if applicable. Likewise, the proposed activities will be coordinated. Chapter 6 will delve more into this specific concern.
- **Climate and environmental responsibility**: even for the non-climate or non-environmental oriented programs, the proposals showed how the proposed activities are assessed using environmental risks and climate change lenses, and in turn, how these activities will address the relevant risk as well as improve the resilience of targeted people, communities, or markets.
- **Sustainability and scalability**: for both development programming and protracted crises, sustainability and scalability are two essential aspects that should be addressed by INGOs in their program design. This is to demonstrate how IDAPs' suggested activities are sustainable, scalable, and can continue after the INGOs leave and the fund expires.

- **Learning and adapting on the levels of projects and confederations**: learning and evidence-based adapting should be outlined from the design phase. This is to inform adjustments made throughout the execution of IDAPs and to share learnings with various organizations at the confederation's level of INGOs
- **Value for money**: proposals should demonstrate cost-effectiveness, and in turn, the cost or targeted entity.

4.4 Alignment with the Donor's Goals

The essence of INGOs' role in implementing IDAPs is to facilitate the connection between donors and targeted communities. As such, the donor is an indispensable stakeholder that must be managed throughout the project's lifespan. This section focuses primarily on the alignment of IDAPs' objectives with the donor's goals, which is mainly related to the program design stage. Chapter 10 will provide a complete set of strategies to employ when managing donors, as noted by Saleh and Karia (2020). This is to address the complexity of IDAPs management in order to maximize value for people's interests, which should not be compromised in any case.

To ensure strategic alignment of IDAPs, objectives and indicators of donors should be addressed proactively. This is not only to meet the original global north development objectives but also because donors have become more sophisticated and demanding with regard to effectiveness, efficiency, and the relevancy of funded issues, all of which are influenced by an "audit culture" in their home countries and with taxpayers (Kloster 2019).

The most recent development of international industrial standards for humanitarian and development actions has made it easier for INGOs to align strategies and projects with donor mandates. This implies that well-developed INGO strategies should already cover the globally agreed-upon goals shared by most international donors, such as the CHS, SDGs, localization, sustainability, and scalability.

It is essential for INGOs to proactively map, consult, and gain buy-in from donors during the strategic development process. This will ensure that INGOs can positively match their IDAPs with donor aims, increasing their competitiveness in receiving funds and reaching out to disadvantaged people and communities all over the world. This approach is preferable to designing and implementing individual programs one by one based on donors' priorities.

Therefore, the availability of well-developed strategies for INGOs means default alignment with most of the donors' mandates and goals. The only remaining part might be rephrasing the indicators used in the proposals or using the verbatim of donors' indicators directly in case it is required.

4.5 Considerations of Project Management Processes

Quality begins with design. Therefore, the earlier sections of this chapter discussed the various strategic alignments of IDAPs in the proposal or design stages. Nevertheless, this alignment will not be put into practice unless it is explicitly incorporated into the PM processes, including planning and implementation.

The project charter is essential for kickstarting a project as it provides authorization for it to take place. With the help of key inputs such as project documents, agreements, business cases, and benefits management plans, the Project Management Institute (PMI) recommends creating this document. Doing so ensures that the project charter strategizes the project and links the agreements with the funder's reasoning for beginning the process to the project's actual implementation. Consequently, it outlines the project's goals and objectives. Once the project charter has been created, project initiation and planning can be started using the charter as a key source of information. This includes gathering the requirements of stakeholders, establishing the scope of the project into definitive work packages, and ensuring the goals and objectives set out in the charter are monitored and controlled.

Saleh and Karia (2020) identified a set of requirements for IDAPs from the conventional PM models. They highlighted the significance of connecting the IDAPs to the strategic objectives of implementing the organization and with longer-term programs. Nevertheless, Saleh and Karia (2022) suggested an adaptive PM model with the aim of putting these requirements into practice. Following the integration of various IDAP strategies into the project charter, they proposed further changes to the communication and resource management processes to ensure effective dissemination of these alignments throughout the IDAP and among stakeholders. They also recommended that organizational and program strategies be included in the job descriptions and performance management of the project teams.

This adaptation of the standard PM models goes beyond the project and establishes an explicit connection with the wider programs, social missions, and visions of INGOs. This was a consensus among the participants interviewed in their field consultations, who agreed that it would allow for better promotion of learning across the project's life cycle and a cumulative experience that could be applied to wider programming. An additional participant commented that this adaptation is more important for INGOs, as it allows them to create more connected projects. She also noted that it helps operationalize the strategic plan for implementing INGO and demonstrate its strategy to donors. According to her, donors "do not fund standalone projects, but cumulative ones." Lastly, one of the participants added that a well-integrated and well-communicated vision and mission would "facilitate the linkages, increasing the impact of the multiple projects that are working under the same organizational strategy."

4.6 Strategic Performance Management

Usually, INGOs have well-established organizational strategies and/or business plans for their operations. Thus, the concepts and proposals for IDAPs are often designed based on these strategies. However, most of these INGOs have difficulty managing their strategic performance, monitoring the advancement of their strategies' successes, and evaluating their collective long-term impacts beyond the individual projects that are generally evaluated to comply with donor contractual requirements. This is especially evident in organizations that adopt project-based structures.

By measuring the cumulative and long-term effects of IDAPs, INGOs can showcase their impact, garner donations, and maintain their ability and accountability to the public, donors, and all stakeholders. To achieve this, concrete and deliberate steps must be taken.

As discussed in Chapter 2, IDAPs are the primary means by which INGOs put their strategic objectives into practice. Consequently, progress toward a strategy should be evaluated on an organizational level at the country missions and federations' levels, covering yearly progress for the strategy's lifetime. Before delving further into strategic performance management, certain prerequisites must be established in addition to having strategized concepts and project design and ensuring the strategic alignments during the implementation of IDAPs as mentioned earlier in this chapter. These include, but are not limited to:

- **Structures follow strategies**: whatever type of structure an INGO has, its organizational structures should be designed to support the organization's strategies. Consequently, a senior manager or board member should be assigned to oversee a specific strategic goal or area of impact outlined in the strategy. This individual should be accountable for reporting on progress toward achieving the said goal or area of impact. This should also include program support objectives such as finance and administration. A Director of Quality should be added to the structure of INGOs to support and facilitate the strategic performance management processes.
- **Strategic key performance indicators**: once the strategies have been developed, it is important to establish Key Performance Indicators (KPIs) that are SMART (Specific, Measurable, Achievable, Relevant, and Timely) and can measure the output, outcome, and impact of all strategic objectives, as well as set reasonable targets. The Head of Mission should lead this process with the assistance of the Director of Quality.
- **Tracking tools**: Progress reporting templates should be created and agreed upon between board members or senior management team members in order to measure the progress of missions in different countries. This also applies to larger INGOs with federated structures. Thus, global tracking and measurement tools should be in place to evaluate the impact of different IDAPs and in-country missions on global strategic objectives.

If the strategic objectives have been clearly set and communicated throughout the organization, and the IDAPs are designed to operationalize these objectives and others that serve the different strategic alignments, with KPIs to measure the objectives and the necessary tools to monitor and report on them, then INGO leadership should be in a strong position to manage the strategic performance process effectively.

The key to successful strategic performance management is the consistent monitoring of progress toward reaching strategic objectives and being able to adjust quickly to any deviations, changes in context, or risks that may arise. However, the frequency of monitoring strategic objectives should depend on the duration of the strategy and the external environment in which the INGOs are operating. For instance, emergency settings vary from stable settings where development and peacebuilding activities are carried out. Generally, quarterly and yearly reporting cycles are widely accepted in various contexts. The rest of this section focuses on three key tools for measuring and reporting longer-term strategic objectives and impacts: quarterly progress reports, annual reports, and program-level impact measurements.

4.6.1 Quarterly Progress Reporting

Typically, the leadership or boards of INGOs gather weekly, bi-weekly, or monthly. No matter the topics of these meetings, it is recommended that one of these meetings at the end of each quarter is devoted to evaluating the progress of strategic key performance indicators (KPIs).

The board members and senior managers should come prepared for this meeting with their input for the quarterly report. This report, and in turn, the discussion, should include the accomplishments in the specified strategic area as emerged from the IDAPs in the in-country mission based on the identified KPIs, along with any successes, setbacks, and the necessary support from other members or from the head of the mission concerning the underachieved targets or anticipated risks.

In general, INGOs operate in turbulent contexts. Therefore, their leaders need to remain mindful of the various contextual elements in their areas of operation, which can be drastically unpredictable. This should be considered during the quarterly discussion on the strategies and/or targets. It is, therefore, recommended to add an agenda item to the quarterly meetings to review these contextual aspects and suggest adaptations to the strategic objectives or KPIs as needed.

4.6.2 Annual Reporting

As part of government control over non-profits, most countries require INGOs to submit annual reports and financial statements to monitor their income and expenses. This is part of the INGOs' financial transparency. However, the leading organizations take a more intentional and sophisticated approach to annual reporting, not only at their headquarters, but also in their in-country missions, in order to demonstrate their operations and advance their business plans alike.

The content of annual reports for INGOs varies depending on the type of operations being conducted. Additionally, the content of such reports may differ between those at the headquarters level and those at in-country mission levels. Here we focus on in-country missions where IDAPs are directly implemented. We will look at the potential aims and benefits of annual reports for INGOs and suggest data points the annual report should be covered, and in turn, to achieve these aims.

The annual report's audience can include all stakeholders of INGOs, such as impacted communities, current and potential donors, partners, staff, headquarters, governmental entities, and the public. As a result, the annual report can be an effective communication tool for a variety of purposes. Most importantly, the annual report should be treated as a formal strategic progress reporting tool. To this end, it should begin by reminding the reader of the INGO's presence in the country and the cumulative figures of reach and impact. It should then set out the current strategic objectives, key targeted KPIs, and achieved figures under these KPIs.

> *"I worked for an organization with a 75-year presence in the country. This INGO is always eager to remind its readers in its annual report of its longstanding presence in the country, as well as its overall reach numbers throughout the years."—one of the authors of this book.*

Good strategies clearly articulate objectives or programmatic impact areas with their Theories of Change (ToC) and pre-determined targets. Reporting on these objectives should be the focus of the annual report, which should compile data from all implemented IDAPs during the year under these program goals. The report should provide quantitative figures of the achieved KPIs and qualitative supporting evidence to illustrate the progress of achievements for these objectives or program goals. This type of measurement is not only advantageous for strategic performance management, but it can also make members of IDAPs proud of their accomplishments and contributions to the organization's program goals.

> *I would tell the story of each programmatic theme in the annual report by combining quantitative and qualitative findings with a success story that provides an example of what we have achieved or are striving to achieve under that theme.—One of the authors of this book.*

When the annual report conveys the story through numerical data, descriptive narratives, and anecdotes, it can be seen as a valuable tool for fundraising efforts. It can be shared with potential donors, made publicly available, and included as part of proposal submission packages.

A common theme throughout the functions and lifecycles of INGOs and IDAPs is "*accountability*." This will be referred to in most chapters of this book. The performance management strategies and reporting tools mentioned above can address accountability from the programmatic side, but accountability from the financial perspective still needs to be addressed in the annual report. Therefore, the annual report should include the annual financial statement of INGO, including revenues and expenses. This basic financial data reporting should be supplemented with more detailed financial figures disaggregated based on the programmatic goals.

Additionally, the annual report can highlight several data points that can include, but are not limited to:

- **Message from the head of mission or country director**: to briefly shed light on the key achievements and challenges of the past year and moving forward.
- **INGO's staff**: including percentages of international and local staff. Similarly, the percentages of several disadvantaged groups, such as women, youth, and those with disabilities.
- **INGO's board members or senior management team members**: this can include a brief biography of the members.
- **Transparency and accountability to targeted people**: including the number, type. It should also include disaggregation of received feedback from community members, mitigation measures for fraud, corruption, and safeguarding, and responsible data management measurements.
- **Organizational and managerial data points**: including key milestones related to the efficiency of operations, quality control and assurance measures, digitization processes, and environmental conversation measures.
- **INGO's supporters**: list of supporters along with their logos in line with their visibility requirements.
- **Acknowledgement or "*thank you*" statement to the supporters**

4.6.3 Program-Level Impact Measurement

In Chapter 7, we will discuss the different dimensions, modalities, and processes of IDAPs evaluations. In this chapter, however, our focus is on the evaluation of longer-term program goals, which aims to measure the impact of INGOs in relation to their strategic objectives and program goals beyond the evaluation of individual IDAPs.

Quality and evidence-based strategic performance management require the measurement of the impact of INGO's program goals beyond the time-phased IDAPs and individual project evaluations. As a rule of thumb, we recommend conducting two impact evaluations for each strategic objective or program goal, unless the program goals are intersected in a manner that necessitates a unified impact evaluation. The first evaluation should take place at the midpoint of the strategic plan lifecycle, while the second should be done at the end.

To enable successful cross-IDAPs evaluations, the leadership of an INGO should ensure the availability of the following prerequisites:

- A ToC for the INGO strategic plan, and a ToC for each program goal.
- A dedicated and perhaps centralized leadership, resources, and commitment to these evaluations.

References

Bayiley YT, Teklu GK (2016) Success factors and criteria in the management of international development projects: evidence from projects funded by the European Union in Ethiopia. Int J Manag Proj Bus 9(3):562–582

Fukuda-Parr S (2016) From the millennium development goals to the sustainable development goals: Shifts in purpose, concept, and politics of global goal setting for development. Gend Dev 24(1):43–52. https://doi.org/10.1080/13552074.2016.1145895

Kloster, M. O. (2019). Why it hurts–Save the children Norway and the dilemmas of 'going global'. In Forum for development studies (Vol. 46, No. 1, pp. 109–130). Routledge.

Saleh FIM, Karia N (2020) Management for international development and aid projects: a new conceptual model. Nonprofit Manag Leadersh 31(2):373–386

Saleh FI, Karia N (2022) Adaptive project management model for the international development and aid projects. Nonprofit Management and Leadership.

Sweis RJ, Saleh FIM, Dahiyat SE, Sweis NJ, Saleh RA, Diab H (2016) Benchmarking of TQM practices in INGOs: a literature review. Benchmarking Int J 23(1):236–261

Chapter 5
Value-Driven Program Design and Fundraising

5.1 Introduction

In Chapter 4, we discussed the importance of strategically designing IDAPs in the proposal and program design stages. To ensure that the project aligns with the organization's broader structures and programs, national plans and priorities, and donor requirements, it is essential to establish the concept and design of the project from the outset to create the maximum strategic value and impact of the IDAPs. Nevertheless, these projects will ultimately be of no value if they do not improve the lives of the people and communities they are intended to benefit. However, some longer-term programs, particularly those that adopt what is called the Market Systems Development (MSD) approach, might delay the strategic alignments of IDAPs after getting the fund. This is done to thoroughly coordinate these initiatives throughout their conception phases. Whatever the stage of strategic alignment, these procedures should not be skipped.

In this chapter, we will delve deeper into program design by looking at it through a value-driven lens, from the perspective of those it is targeting, and the nature of the activities involved. We will also consider the critical success factors of good designs, needs-based and opportunity-based approaches, fundraising elements, and how they intersect with MEAL functions.

Suggestion: Given the significance of IDAP's better aims, the most crucial and mandatory alignment must be with the needs of targeted individuals and communities, particularly their well-being, expectations, inspirations, and growth. Firstly, we will discuss how to make IDAPs proposals and program design well-informed with the needs and priorities of targeted people. Then, the three kinds of opportunity-based program design will be discussed before concluding with the MEAL aspects that need to be incorporated into the ultimate quality of program design.

F. I. Mahmoud Saleh and N. Karia, *Value-driven Management for International Development and Aid Projects*, https://doi.org/10.1007/978-981-97-3666-9_5

5.2 Needs-Based Program Design

A proposal is a tool used by INGOs to demonstrate the ability and approaches to respond to identified objectives in donors' calls for action. These calls typically state the business case and the problems that need to be addressed in the proposals. Therefore, to be considered for funding. However, not all good proposals receive funding, as other underlying political or dynamic factors can come into play. While managing relationships with donors to serve fundraising efforts will be discussed in Chapter 10, this chapter focuses on the technical quality of proposals from the perspective of their potential benefit for program participants.

A good proposal or implementation strategy should start with an evidence-based identification of the gaps, vulnerabilities, and needs of the targeted people, communities, market systems, or areas. This should be based on published data from trusted sources, such as government censuses and UN agencies, and involve consultation with the potential recipients of the proposed activities and other relevant stakeholders (Baker et al. 2013; Alam and Baidya 2019). It should also be based on the sound needs assessments, gender and inclusion analysis, conflict sensitivity analysis, and market analysis.

Some proposals might need specific consultations with a sample of targeted people. However, INGOs with a strong presence in their areas of operation should regularly assess the needs of those areas or conduct rapid needs assessments once emergencies emerge rather than wait for requests from donors. The most informed INGOs should be seen as a reliable source of knowledge on the areas in which they work, so they can influence and inform donors' priorities and strategies. This is especially important in humanitarian responses, where resources and timeframes for program design and implementation are limited.

Evidence-based needs are the most vital element of successful proposals. To justify interventions, it is essential to identify the target population and their needs accurately. These needs should be broken down into the smallest geographical areas and communities. Moreover, gender, age, and social inclusion analysis must be employed to guarantee the inclusiveness of IDAPs and ensure no one is left behind. One way to accomplish this is through gender and age analysis, which evaluates the particular vulnerabilities of disadvantaged people and those with specific needs regarding access to and control of services.

Proposals that target different communities or sensitive tribal or ethnic contexts should be accompanied by a conflict sensitivity analysis to assess and address any potential negative risks arising from the proposed intervention or from targeting certain communities distinctively from other communities. This analysis should consider power dynamics, control over resources, and the probability of conflicts resulting from these dynamics. For example, proposals targeting refugee communities in camps should consider and address the needs and potential adverse views of the hosting communities around these camps (CHS 2019).

5.3 Opportunity-Based Program Design

Scholars and practitioners have acknowledged the wide variety of contexts in which INGOs operate and implement IDAPs as a key factor in their complexity (Saleh and Karia 2020). For instance, humanitarian INGOs may need to assess the needs and plan on the fly, whereas more stable contexts such as development programming, peacebuilding programming, or market systems development programming offer more opportunities and the luxury of time for INGOs to identify needs, gaps, and potential opportunities for those in need. As a result, practitioners often refer to this type of programming as "opportunity-based" rather than "needs-based."

In humanitarian contexts, needs assessments, rapid needs assessments, gender and age analysis, and (to a lesser extent) conflict sensitivity are commonly used to identify the needs of target populations. However, other tools are necessary to identify potential opportunities in more stable settings. These may include, but are not limited to, market and market system analysis, value chain analysis, stakeholder analysis, sustainability and scalability analysis, and the Theory of Change (ToC). These tools are utilized to inform the longer-term development plans of IDAPs that have rolling waves and adaptive designs of interventions.

Opportunity-based assessments are widely employed in development programming, peacebuilding, macro-economics, and MSD programming in order to achieve longer-term, sustainable impacts and promote systemic changes to support people's growth and improve the quality of macro systems. These objectives may include, but are not limited to, behavior and social change, economic development, enhanced infrastructures, leverage of the market systems' supportive functions, and support of governmental systems and sectoral ecosystems.

It is not unusual for long-term international projects to utilize the initial year of IDAPs for evaluating the system's gaps and potential sustainable enhancements. In this book, we recommend structuring opportunity-based evaluations into three levels. Firstly, the agency level of focused persons or entities. Secondly, the level of relations and behaviors, and lastly, the structural or system level. The rest of this section will discuss these three levels of opportunity-level assessments. We borrowed this multi-layer approach from both CARE's Gender Equality Framework (Ruano-Chamorro et al. 2022), the MSD approach (Humphrey 2014), and system theory.

5.3.1 Agency-Level Assessments

Agency-level assessments are conducted with the aim of setting startup values for the data points related to the capacity and condition of targeted entities, which may be individuals or businesses. These assessments also seek to identify opportunities to increase self-competence, autonomy, and growth prospects for these entities and consequently provide information for directing interventions that target them.

Value-added agency-level assessments should analyze and disaggregate their targeted data points into age, gender, social, and entities with special needs. This should be accompanied by an exploration of correlations and intersectionality between the different data points in order to highlight any significant differences among the sub-groups and any potential dependencies of data points on each other.

Practically, it is not straightforward to accurately target entities through agency-level assessments, as the participants in these assessments are often not beneficiaries of IDAPs. The findings from these assessments can be used to establish a "control group" for comparison with the targeted entities. Additionally, the current state of the targeted entities in long-term IDAPs can be subject to contextual effects or the cumulative interventions of the IDAP itself. Therefore, agency-level assessments will require regular supplementary assessments for the identified and onboarded targeted entities. This type of agency-level assessment is known as a "rolling baseline," which provides more accurate, timely, and phased insights into the current state of the entities targeted by the IDAPs.

5.3.2 Relations Level Assessments

Grounded by the system theory, the essence of development programming lies in its ability to create sustainable outcomes. Yet, without a human-centered approach to transformation, true sustainability cannot be realized (Klaniecki et al. 2016). The system theory models complex entities by abstracting structural details and focusing on the dynamics that define the system's functions, properties, and relationships. This approach is based on the interaction of multiple components (Laszlo and Krippner 1998). Therefore, this book recognized the relations-level assessments as the second layer of opportunity-based assessments that should be done together with agency-level assessments toward ensuring value-added IDAPs.

Regardless of the purpose of IDAPs, relationship-level assessments of international development programming should first identify the stakeholders or targeted system actors. This should include identifying power holders, perspectives, and attitudes toward intended behavior changes. For instance, IDAPs with gender-transformative goals should not only focus on women and girls but should also engage men and boys in this layer of opportunity-based assessments. This will enable a better understanding and analysis of their perceptions, and the appropriate action can then be taken. The same applies to economic development programming, in which the perceptions and behaviors of the different actors in the market should be analyzed and targeted by the IDAPs, along with the agency-level interventions of poor people or businesses.

An agency-level assessment can serve as both an analytical tool and an early intervention for changing behaviors and power dynamics. Data collection for this purpose, which involves bringing together stakeholders and system actors, can also foster self-reflection and positive interactions, provided it is done correctly.

5.3.3 Structure-Level Assessments

Structure-level assessments seek to influence the structural aspects or gaps that limit the achievement of a particular development goal, social system, or market system. This is done in order to bring about permanent, sustainable, and multiplied changes that ultimately benefit the people, communities, or entities affected. This type of assessment is usually referred to by practitioners as system-level assessments. It is important, however, to note that the IDAP should not be based on a single-level assessment but rather on all three levels of assessments.

To that purpose, system-level assessments analyze primary or secondary data to identify the underlying sources of vulnerabilities affecting targeted entities or to address the insufficient performance of particular social or economic systems. For example, when it comes to IDAPs that seek to bring about gender-transformative changes, the following data points should be taken into consideration:

- How the relevant policies and laws on women and girls' issues affect the access and control of these targeted groups over resources. Such as ownership laws, employment policies, and education systems.
- Relevel social norms that affect women and girls.
- The infrastructure might affect the access of women and girls to resources.
- System actors such as community leaders who have the power to grant or prevent access to women and girls over resources, as well as the distribution of power across the social system.
- The availability and multiplicity of alternative channels for women and girls to access and control resources.

The MSD approach is a major form of international development programming that is heavily reliant on system-level assessments. The primary objective of this approach is to improve the lives of those in poverty. To achieve this goal, interventions at the system level should be informed by a "market system analysis," which considers the following data points:

- The core exchange value in the system.
- The provider and consumer of the identified exchanged value.
- Identification of system actors and core functions between the first supply and ultimate demand.
- The policies, norms, and laws that govern the system and exchange of value in the market system.
- The relevant supporting systems. Such as, but not limited to, infrastructures, transportation systems, delivery systems, financial and payment systems, and water and electricity sources.

The ultimate outcome of the system-level assessments can be in the form of system maps that show all of the data points mentioned above along with traffic-light-like determinations of what works well, what needs to be improved, and what is not functioning across the system. The IDAPs and their implementation strategies, therefore, use these maps and design and implement the interventions of IDAP accordingly.

In some cases, such as MSD programming in fragile contexts, practitioners may not be able to wait for the three levels of assessments to be completed before implementation. This is because the gaps or urgent needs of the entities or market system are already known to a certain extent. As a result, direct interventions can be started with only one or even no assessments at all.

In this chapter, we explore the needs-based assessments as well as the three types of opportunity-based assessments that should be conducted during program design. These assessments provide a comprehensive overview of the requirements of the target groups, the behaviors of stakeholders and market actors, and the current state of the social or market system. The next chapter will discuss how to incorporate and utilize the results of these assessments throughout the life cycle of the IDAP.

5.4 Linkages with Monitoring, Evaluation, and Learning (MEAL)

The needs-based and opportunity-based assessments can give a comprehensive overview of the necessities of targeted entities and systems. However, it is important to consider the newly gained knowledge from past programs when designing a value-added IDAP (Vaughan et al. 2017). Therefore, the following aspects and data points need to be considered to enhance the quality of IDAPs' designs:

- The recommendations emerged from the impact evaluations of similar IDAPs. Therefore, providing proof of the effectiveness of the proposed implementation modalities.
- Development of IDAPs key performance indicators and logical frameworks based on the previously tested ToCs as well as pre-identified or mandatory indicators of donors or implementing INGO.
- Identify the risks of fraud and corruption, misuse of resources and power, and sexual harassment, exploitation, and abuse.
- The learning agenda includes learning questions, learning events, and processes of using and sharing learnings as part of intended adaptive management procedures.

Strengthening IDAP's design with these MEAL aspects will not only rationalize the proposed interventions and implementation modalities but also increase the chances of successful and winning submissions. In Chapter 7, we will unpack the management of MEAL functions throughout the IDAP's lifecycle.

References

Alam M, Baidya EU (2019) Empowering the urban poor through participatory planning process: A case from Jhenaidah, Bangladesh. International Journal of Contemporary Urban Affairs 3(2):47–54

Baker J, Sanghvi T, Hajeebhoy N, Martin L, Lapping K (2013) Using an evidence-based approach to design large-scale programs to improve infant and young child feeding. Food Nutr Bull 34(3_suppl2):S146–S155

Core Humanitarian Standard (CHS), (2019) Core humanitarian standard on quality and accountability. https://corehumanitarianstandard.org/

Humphrey J (2014) Market systems approaches. https://beamexchange.org/uploads/filer_public/b2/3a/b23a3505-e3f1-4f63-8c0c-aeb35a763f91/beamliteraturereview.pdf

Klaniecki K, Wuropulos K, Hager CP (2016) Behaviour change for sustainable development. In: Leal Filho, W (ed) Encyclopedia of Sustainability in Higher Education, pp 1–10

Laszlo A, Krippner S (1998) Systems theories: Their origins, foundations, and development. Advances in Psychology-Amsterdam- 126:47–76

Ruano-Chamorro C, Lau J, Lawless S, Cohen P, Deering K, McDougall C (2022) Advancing gender equality in coral reef social-ecological systems. https://careevaluations.org/wp-content/uploads/WIF35_ARC_WorldFish_CARE-_-GTAs-and-coral-reef-systems.pdf

Saleh FIM, Karia N (2020) Management for international development and aid projects: A new conceptual model. Nonprofit Manag Leadersh 31(2):373–386

Vaughan N, Reali A, Stenbom S, Van Vuuren MJ, MacDonald D (2017) Blended learning from design to evaluation: International case studies of evidence-based practice. Online Learning 21(3):103–114

Part II
Core Elements of Managing IDAPs

Chapter 6
Management of People of Concern, Targeted Communities, and Partners

6.1 Introduction

In Part I, we discussed the need for IDAPs to create a new PM paradigm. To address the nuances and complexities inherent in these types of projects, we explored the various strategic alignments required and how to strategically plan for them in the design phase. This includes aligning and justifying interventions based on the needs of those affected and the available opportunities for improving the situation of affected entities or the performance of targeted systems.

In Part II, we introduce the core elements of value-driven management for IDAPs, as well as the functional domains and processes that must be managed as part of the PM lifecycle. The chapter outlines the practical applications of how to manage the needs and expectations of targeted people, communities, and partnerships within global localization commitments in an inclusive and evidence-based manner.

6.2 Management of Needs, Participation, and Inclusion

Unlike most PM standards, only a few custom methodologies for development projects, such as PMD Pro 2nd edition, have been designed to partially meet the industry-specific requirements of IDAPs (Saleh and Karia 2020). The purpose of this book is to introduce how to manage these specific types of projects and add value to them for the benefit of targeted people.

The core value added by IDAPs, and thus PM considerations, lies in the management of people's needs, participation, and inclusion. Based on the summarized Ph.D. thesis of Saleh and Karia (2022), this chapter outlines the PM processes required to meet this superior value of IDAPs, along with the inputs, tools, techniques, and outputs of these processes. Furthermore, we provide three processes that practitioners can adopt in any PM lifecycle, domain, or knowledge area, as well as for any

F. I. Mahmoud Saleh and N. Karia, *Value-driven Management for International Development and Aid Projects*, https://doi.org/10.1007/978-981-97-3666-9_6

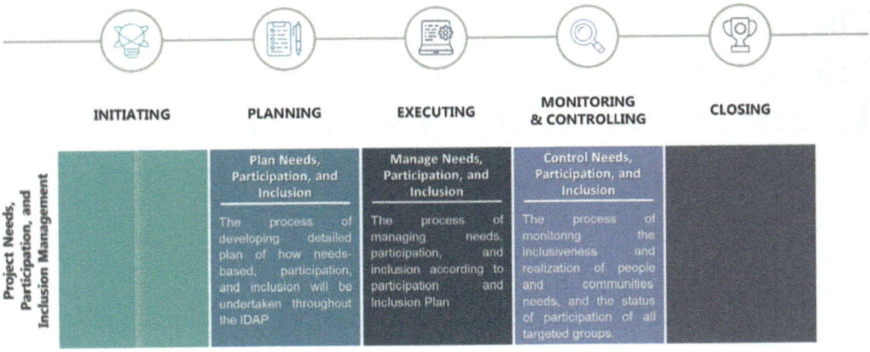

Fig. 6.1. Project needs, participation, and inclusion management

sector-specific humanitarian or development programming. The rest of this section describes these three processes that aim to plan, manage, and control the needs, participation, and inclusion of IDAPs. See Fig. 6.1.

6.2.1 Plan Needs, Participation, and Inclusion

This process should be part of the PM Plan and aims to develop a detailed plan for how needs-based, opportunity-based, inclusive participation, engagement, diversity, the inclusion of marginalized groups, and the assurance of sufficient disaggregation of data collected from targeted people will be undertaken throughout the project lifecycle.

The key outputs of this process can be in the form of three subsidiary plans, as follows:

- **Needs and Opportunities Register**: a list of identified needs to be addressed or opportunities to be pursued by the IDAP. This subsidiary plan will be developed during the planning phase of the project and used by the MEL functions. Therefore, it is the foundation on which these processes build the data collection tools to monitor the progress of achieving the identified needs, opportunities, and evaluate their realizations in the different kinds of evaluations or reviews of IDAPs.
- **Participation and Inclusion Plan**: This plan outlines how age and gender groups will be engaged and included in the implementation, monitoring, controlling, and evaluation of the project.
- **Data Disaggregation Plan**: The roles of disaggregation can include gender (female/male), family structures (FHH/MHH), age groups (youth, children, and elderlies), nationalities, areas, and sectors.

To develop these plans, the necessary ingredients and prerequisites should be available and utilized accordingly, with any that do not already exist needing to be developed:

- **Project Documents, Including Proposals or Agreements.**
- **Needs Assessments.**
- **Gender and Inclusion Analysis.**
- **Market Assessments.**
- **Benefits Management Plans (if applicable).**

Therefore, the PM team can use these ingredients to come up with the outputs mentioned above using one or more of the following tools and techniques:

- **Participatory Design of Activities**: to conduct design consultations with different target groups. These consultations should include all the targeted gender and age groups as well as the different community parts, system actors, and stakeholders.
- **Participatory Analysis**: if the different types of assessments were not part of the proposal development stage, they should be undertaken as part of this process together with the targeted groups.
- **Gender, Resilience, Inclusive Governance, Sustainability, or Environmental Markers**.
- **Data Gathering, Analysis, and Representation**.
- **Expert Judgment**: such as gender or environmental experts.

6.2.2 Manage Needs, Participation, and Inclusion

During the implementation of IDAPs, the PM team must manage the requirements and opportunities stated in the needs and opportunities register. Additionally, they must manage participation and inclusion plans, as well as data disaggregation plans. This process will make use of all the generated outputs and subsidiary plans developed during the process of planning for needs, participation, and inclusion.

To achieve this goal, a variety of tools and techniques can be employed, such as data gathering, data analysis, data representation, information management systems, and expert judgment. As a result, this process can lead to the following actions:

- As part of the iterative process of identifying and developing needs and opportunities, the PM team will need to regularly revisit the needs and opportunities register in order to document any newly identified needs and opportunities, as well as to update the status of their realization.
- Change requests to the other PM processes, such as but not limited to amendments of scope of work, schedules, budgets, staffing, resources, or communications.
- Changes to the project's agreements or sub-agreements.
- Amendments to the needs and opportunities register or the project's risk register.

6.2.3 Control Needs, Participation, and Inclusion

In order to monitor the inclusiveness, participation, and realization of identified needs under IDAP, the PM team requires an additional process, "Control Needs, Participation, and Inclusion." Specifically, this process aims to monitor the extent to which identified needs in the needs and opportunities register are being met and to track the implementation of participation and inclusion plans, as well as data disaggregation plans. This will enable the team to take corrective or preventive action, as needed, to ensure that these baselines stay on track.

Accordingly, the quality of execution of this process requires being informed by the following inputs: PM plan with all its subsidiary plans, project documents, work performance data, and feedback from targeted people or entities, and any available organizational process assets within the implementing INGO that might include templates, lessons learned from previous IDAPs, and pre-identified technical checklists and markers. The PM team can then utilize these inputs, with the aid of information management systems and expert judgments, to collect and analyze the data to generate participation and inclusion measurements or indicators and suggest changes to the PM plan and its subsidiary plans.

6.2.4 Added Value of Managing Needs, Participation, and Inclusion

According to the primary findings of Saleh and Karia (2022), the practitioners have agreed that these processes have a positive effect on the success of their IDAPs. This, however, is because of the specific and intangible nature of IDAPs, as these processes support the notion of self-determination and do-no-harm approaches, which are considered part of the overall accountability of INGOs to their donors and targeted communities alike. Some practitioners cited that the "*project's participants will feel that they own the project and are accountable for the success and lasting impact of the project, which will return to them.*" The positive effect also extends to the management of IDAP itself, as cited by another practitioner, in which "*the early inclusion of targeted communities in the early stages of planning will facilitate any adaptations throughout the project life cycle in case any unintended matters happen*" and "*will reduce the number of changes and their associated costs during the project implementation,*" another practitioner said. In particular, when the "*cultural aspects and needs of people with special needs are captured through these newly added processes.*" One practitioner added that these processes will "*help them to best understand the needs of targeted communities and will allow managers of IDAPs not only to understand the needs concerning the current implemented IDAP but also to inform future IDAPs.*" As such, "*participation and inclusion became a mandatory requirement but not optional for the majority of donors*" and a condition to win the donations.

6.3 Plan, Manage, and Control Community Leadership

Saleh and Karia (2020) have identified the sensitivity of local cultures and differences, local capacities, the complexity of needs and expectations, and the relevancy of IDAPs' interventions to the local realities as key complexities of IDAPs that need to be addressed when managing IDAPs. This, however, is aligned with the sustainability principles as well as with the temporary presence of INGOs in the operating areas. Therefore, Saleh and Karia (2022) have proposed three processes that need to be considered as part of the overall stakeholder management domain of IDAPs' PM. These three processes are Plan Community Leadership, Manage Community Leadership, and Control Community Leadership. See Fig. 6.2.

The rest of this section describes the three proposed processes that should be managed intentionally as part of overall IDAPs' stakeholder management to ensure community leadership on the IDAPs.

6.3.1 *Plan Community Leadership*

This process aims to identify potential community leaders and structures and develop detailed community leadership plans, including capacity development and preparedness for further risks. Therefore, the IDAP's PM team should review the project charter, project management plan, scopes of works stakeholder register, project agreements, and proposal, enterprise environmental factors, and any available templates or processes within the implementing INGOs to develop the following plans and outputs:

- **Identification of Potential Community Leaders and Structures.**
- **Community Leadership Plan.**
- **Plan(s) for Capacity Building.**

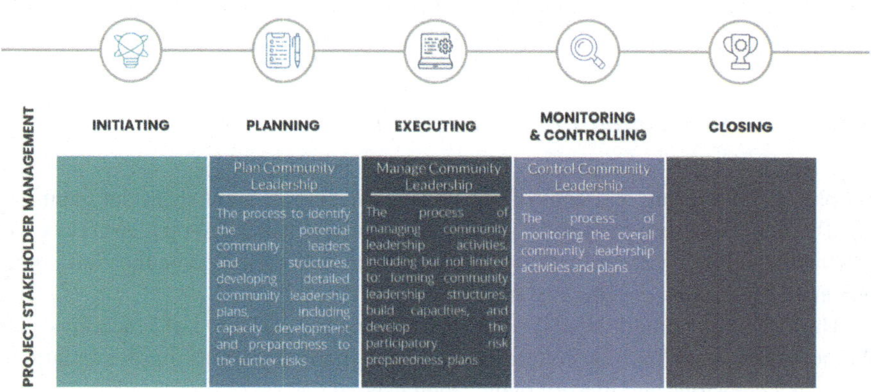

Fig. 6.2. Management community leadership

- **Plan(s) for Community Preparedness.**
- **Potential Updates and Changes to the PM Plan and Project's Documents.**

To that end, the IDAP's PM team can rely on expert judgment, data gathering, analysis, representation techniques, and meetings.

6.3.2 Manage Community Leadership

The community leadership should be managed throughout the project based on the outputs from the planning process. These outputs might be initially stated in the planning phase and can be further elaborated during implementation, as is the case with the agile and rolling wave approaches of PM.

Management of community leadership entails, but is not limited to, forming community leadership structures, building their capacities, and developing participatory risk preparedness plans through meetings, expert judgments, data gathering and analysis, workshops, and training activities. This, however, should be done based on the PM plan (mainly the community leadership plan), project documents (stakeholder register, needs register), enterprise environmental factors, and any available organizational process assets.

As a result of this process, several forms of community structures can be formed. These structures could take the form of community committees, women or youth leadership councils, or community representatives for the purpose of engagement in formal or non-formal activities, such as facilitation, outreach, or policy change such as public–private dialogues or social accountability systems. As such, this process will lead to the creation of risk preparedness plans and further updates and revisions to IDAP's management plans and documents.

The management of community leadership should be approached wisely to ensure the successful mobilization of community structures. To do so effectively, it is essential to have field staff who are knowledgeable about the local culture, have effective communication and interpersonal skills, and are capable of working as part of a team.

6.3.3 Control Community Leadership

As part of monitoring and controlling IDAPs, the project's management team will need to monitor the progress and realization of community leadership plans. They will also need to take corrective or preventive actions as needed to update the community leadership plans and community structures accordingly.

The PM team should depend on their interpersonal skills to hold meetings with the necessary stakeholders, collect and examine data concerning implementations, and make decisions and modify plans when needed.

6.3.4 Added Value of Planning, Managing, and Controlling Community Leadership

Based on the primary validations of Saleh and Karia (2022), the practitioners have agreed that the community leadership processes are valid and very important. Therefore, community ownership and the attraction of community leaders are essential aspects of mitigating community resistance to the IDAPs and ensuring their success, as said by one of the participants. Similarly, without validating the outcomes of IDAPs through community leaders, the IDAPs will not be successful and sustainable. On top of that, community leadership started to be required from donors and local governments alike, she added.

One of the participants indicated that this adaptation might be more applicable for development projects. Applying it to humanitarian projects might be difficult because of the lack of resources for these projects. However, another participant showed an opposing view of this opinion. She indicated that these processes are important even in humanitarian contexts, such as the refugee camps, where the IDAPs aim to prepare the refugees for their durable solutions.

However, the practitioners argued that the quality implementation of the community leadership process and the avoidance of any potential fraud or harm to the targeted people required clear identification of the selection criteria of community leaders as well as clear terms of reference for the community leadership leaders that identify the precise roles and responsibilities for community leaders, particularly if they will have any role in distributing humanitarian assistance. Similarly, explicitly consider regular communication with the community leaders as a key tool and technique under the "Manage Community Leadership" and "Control Community Leadership" process.

6.4 Management of Partnerships for Sustainability

As we discussed in Chapter 2, the new holistic paradigm of IDAPs' management requires considering the relationship with local partners for sustainability. This aspect has been widely advocated in the literature on INGOs partnerships, particularly when it comes to building local capacities (Ika and Donnelly 2017), localization of humanitarian aid (Fiddian-Qasmiyeh and Pacitto 2019), sustaining the development outcomes (Bloomfield et al. 2017), relying on the local knowledge during crisis times (Awasthy et al. 2019), ensuring the ultimate community ownership of projects (Bayiley and Teklu 2016), and harnessing the profound understanding and outreach capabilities of local partners (Boyer and Kolpakov 2018). Sweis et al. (2016) have indicated the importance of forming long-term relationships based on quality selection criteria for sustainability. Additionally, to respect the reciprocity of these partnerships (Olawoore and Kamruzzaman 2019). Yet, these long-term partnerships should include the development of local actors as the first respondents to the crises (Lassa 2019).

Partnerships should also incorporate the standards of quality and accountability into the procurement and grant management processes, build partners' capacities, and continuously support them in this regard (Sweis et al. 2016). Therefore, the likelihood of securing and retaining donors' funds can increase while benefiting from such partnerships between INGO and local partners (Arhin et al. 2018). Accordingly, it is not an option to manage partnerships among IDAPs as an integral part of IDAP's management and closure processes for sustainability after the project's end. To that end, the management of the partnerships should be treated explicitly under the overall stakeholder management of IDAPs. Saleh and Karia (2022), however, proposed a set of considerations to meet this aim. The rest of this section discusses these considerations and how to operationalize them within IDAP's management or intervention cycles. See Fig. 6.3.

Through the "Identity Stakeholder Process," the local partners of the project should be documented along with the level of their commitment, focal points, interests, and power analysis (a new tool to be added to Identify Stakeholders process and, in turn, an output—"partners register" for this process). The partner register might be used for non-local partners as well. Local partners' identification should be based on quality-based criteria and should prioritize these partnerships that can achieve the global localization agenda. Additionally, the maturity level of the current

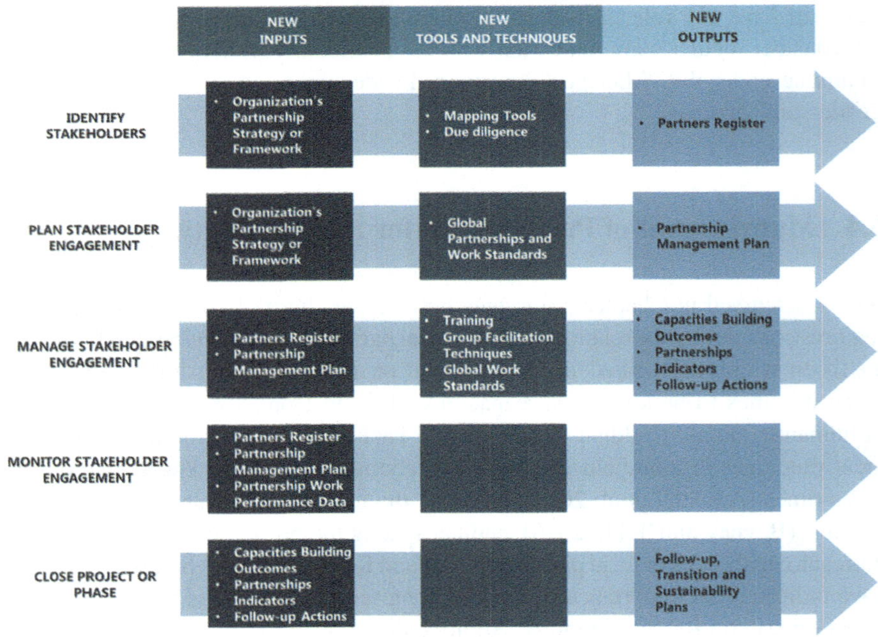

Fig. 6.3. Managing IDAPs partnerships within stakeholder management

partnerships should be identified to inform the planning of capacity building and execution of partnership activities accurately.

As part of the planning stakeholder engagement process, IDAP's team should look at the project charter, which provides the rationale and linkage with the INGO's partnership strategies or frameworks. Likewise, the project team should build engagement plans for stakeholders based on the developed and continuously evolved partner register. To do so, several tools and techniques can be adopted in order to identify and plan the objectives, outcomes, indicators, governance of partnerships, and ways of working with the local partners, including the roles and responsibilities for building partners' capacities and maintaining a long-term relationship with them beyond the project. Also, the global work standards of quality and accountability are to be identified to build the capacities of local partners. Given the absence of globally agreed-upon standards for working with partners, the IDAP's team should brainstorm to determine the required activities for building the capacity of partners concerning the international standards of quality and accountability. In this regard, the "STRENGTHENING NONPROFITS: Manage Stakeholder Engagement" framework is suggested, providing guidance on establishing and managing partnerships. This guidance can be used in all stakeholder management processes.

The planning of partners' engagement should lead to the development of partners' management plan, as it can lead to updating and revising the project management plan (resource management plan, cost management plan, scope management plan, M&E plan, risk management plan, etc.), and updating project documents updates (stakeholder register, partners register, risk register, etc.).

Based on the "Partnership Register" and "Partners Management Strategy", the IDAP's managers should manage the relationship with the local partners, communicate with them, address any concerns, and ensure that the partnerships' desired goals are met. This process will be revealed in changes to the project management plan, amendments to project documents, and updates on the partners' register using the partners' register, partners' management plan, and by conducting training, group facilitation techniques, and global work standards. Lastly, the management of partners' engagement can lead to changes in partners' registers and partnership management plans.

At the end of the IDAP, the resulting outcomes and indicators of partnership activities and capacity building should be documented during the closing project or phase to inform broader organizational partnership strategies or frameworks. Similarly, it can be used as a guide to develop any transition or sustainability plans if required for the current project.

Based on the primary validations of Saleh and Karia (2022), the practitioners have confirmed the importance of partnerships for these projects (Ika and Donnelly 2017) and for the global localization agenda (Fiddian-Qasmiyeh and Pacitto 2019) to sustain the development outcomes (Bloomfield et al. 2017). All the consulted practitioners indicated that this adaptation to the standard PM methodologies is valid and very important. However, this is because "*almost all of our projects are implemented through partners,*" as said by one participant. Furthermore, it is a core donor requirement for the IDAPs and should be part of the overall exit strategies of the INGOs. Furthermore, the practitioners suggested the following further considerations:

- To assess the capacities of potential partners as part of the Identify Stakeholders process. This, however, can be done through partners' capacity assessments, organizational self-assessment (OSA), and due diligence.
- To reach "agreements" with partners as part of the planning stakeholder engagement process. Therefore, all the detailed guidelines and implementation details should be stated, with the understanding that the agreements can be reached prior to the project's start date, either during the initiation, planning, or execution phases, as mentioned by participants.
- Conduct partnership reviews to monitor the stakeholder engagement process. Therefore, assess what went well and what needs to be improved, and gather the lessons learned accordingly.

6.5 Management of Coordination and Complementation

Competition between INGOs is driven by the decrease in funds compared to the rising needs and numbers of vulnerable people (Egger 2018). This can result in tension between organizations or alliances, as well as a race to establish a presence in affected areas with local NGOs (Martinez and Cooper 2017). INGOs may also be pressured to pursue donor-friendly approaches, which could lead to a loss of their assumed positive heterogeneous nature (Davis 2019). However, competition between INGOs also encourages them to improve their processes and performance. Ahmed and Abdullahi (2017) suggest that INGOs should be encouraged to provide improvements in order to compete with existing organizations and new organizations that are quickly developing.

Recent research suggests that directing funds to local NGOs can offer a number of advantages; this has led to increased competition between INGOs and local NGOs. Many donors, however, prefer to avoid the complexity of managing multiple contracts and to shift the risk of working with inexperienced local organizations to INGOs. INGOs often compete for contracts, which can have negative effects on vulnerable people. These organizations tend to take easy and short routes to target and program rather than addressing deeper, more complex needs. This reduces the relevance, effectiveness, and sustainability of IDAPs. INGOs have also shifted their strategies to meet donor interests and preferences instead of centering their plans around the needs of people, which is advocated by the CHS.

Competition and coordination are two sides of the same coin when it comes to the work of INGOs in crisis contexts. While collaboration is key to successful service delivery and assistance, coordination can be difficult due to a lack of understanding or agreement between organizations. Additionally, INGOs must also be mindful of local government policies and coordinate with inter-governmental organizations. If INGOs provide services to vulnerable communities without considering the role of government, they risk creating a dependency on their services, which could prevent the achievement of Sustainable Development Goals. In countries such as Turkey and Jordan, INGOs must partner with national organizations and have their IDAPs approved by the Ministry of Planning and International Cooperation in order to implement their projects.

Coordination is a fundamental part of the industry and involves planning and executing interventions to protect vulnerable people. However, this process is not without its challenges. Oliver-Smith (2019) identified several issues, such as deciding who should lead and how, the capacity of the host government, the structure of organizations, power dynamics, prioritizing partnership over results, and accountability issues. In 2016, the World Humanitarian Summit resulted in the "Grand Bargain" Agreement, a commitment by international donors and humanitarian organizations to ten goals. These goals focus on increasing coordination, reducing duplication, improving joint assessments and participation, harmonizing reporting, localizing, and increasing engagement between humanitarian and development organizations.

Scholars agree that INGOs need to improve the performance and coordination of their IDAPs in order to increase their efficiency of funds and quality of service, as well as maintain successful outcomes. To achieve this, a PM methodology should be implemented that considers the necessary processes for the coordination requirements of IDAPs. (Saleh and Karia 2020). Based on the work of Saleh and Karia (2022), the rest of this section, therefore, provides the required processes that need to be considered as part of any PM methodology to meet the coordination requirements of IDAP. Therefore, identifying local actors, other actors, and coordination platforms in the operations areas can be done as part of "Identify Stakeholders." One of the outcomes of this process might be in the form of a list of who does what (4Ws). Accordingly, three processes are suggested, including planning, managing, and controlling coordination and complementation. See Fig. 6.4.

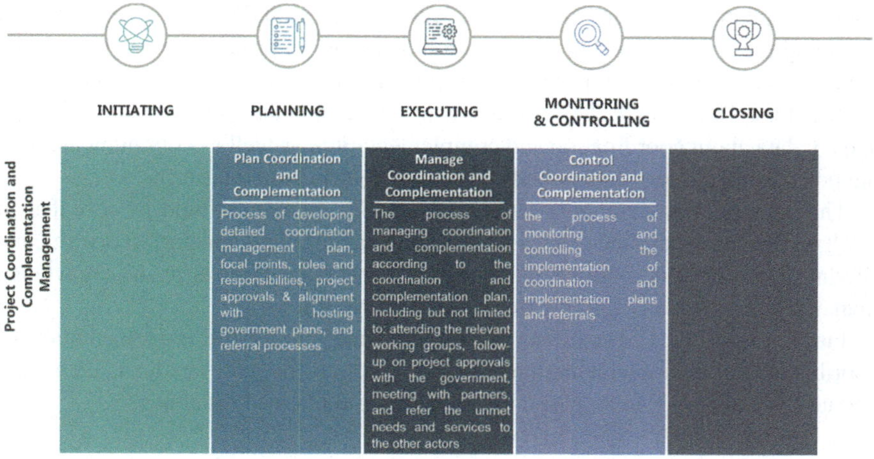

Fig. 6.4. Project coordination and complementation management

6.5.1 Plan Coordination and Complementation

This process of developing a detailed coordination management plan, focal points, roles and responsibilities, project approvals, and alignment with hosting government plans and referral processes based on the project charter, stakeholders register (with a list of actors and 4Ws), staffing management plan, enterprise environmental factors, and organizational process assets of the implementation INGO.

By using the inputs mentioned above, the IDAP's team should gather and analyze the required data, review the governmental plans, analyze who does what, review the relevant coordination platforms, consult and meet experts and relevant stakeholders to take a decision toward the development of the following outputs:

- Coordination Management Plan, a plan for engaging the relevant inter-agency working groups.
- Plan for coordination with other INGOs.
- Identification of the focal points based on their technical areas, including their roles and responsibilities.
- Plan for approval and the reporting process of the project.
- Referral Processes.
- Updates on the PM plan, project documents, and organizational process assets as needed.

6.5.2 Manage and Control Coordination and Complementation

During the implementation of IDAPs, the PM team should manage coordination and complementation according to the project charter, coordination and complementation plan, referral processes, and stakeholder register. This includes, but is not limited to, attending the relevant working groups, following-up on project approvals with the government, meeting with partners, and referring the unmet needs and services to other actors. To that end, the team needs to collect and analyze the required inter-agency data about coordination and complementation, as well as communicate with the potential and already identified partners or coordination platforms.

The management of coordination and complementation should be revealed in work performance data and can lead to updating the PM plans and project documents, sharing lessons learned, minutes of meetings, and contributions to the knowledge management systems within the implementing INGOs.

Furthermore, the PM team should monitor and control the implementation of coordination and complementation plans and referrals, in order to adjust, adapt, and update relevant plans, in response to deviations and planned baselines.

6.5.3 *Added Value of Managing Coordination and Complementation*

The practitioners who have been consulted by Saleh and Karia (2022) regarding the management of IDAP's coordination and complementation have agreed that this aspect plays an essential role in the success of IDAPs, as it allows them to target more people and provides specialized services and assistance to them. Further, it is aligned with the donors' preferences to support the collective actions and perhaps a "*mandatory requirement for several donors to avoid duplication and service provision,*" as added by one practitioner. Similarly, it is aligned with the global commitment to "localization" if undertaken with local actors, as highlighted by another practitioner. Finally, practitioners also indicated the importance of this adaptation to multiply the impact of IDAPs. They further stressed the importance of regular revisions of the 4Ws and the governmental plans.

References

Ahmed S, Abdullahi AM (2017) Leadership and project success in development sector. Journal of Economics & Management 30:5–19

Arhin AA, Kumi E, Adam MAS (2018) Facing the bullet? Non-governmental organisations'(NGOs') Responses to the changing aid landscape in Ghana. VOLUNTAS: Int J Volunt Nonprofit Organ 29(2): 348–360

Awasthy P, Gopakumar KV, Gouda SK, Haldar T (2019) Trust in humanitarian operations: a content analytic approach for an Indian NGO. Int J Prod Res 57(9):2626–2641

Bayiley YT, Teklu GK (2016) Success factors and criteria in the management of international development projects. Int J Manag Proj Bus 9(3):562–582

Bloomfield G, Bucht K, Martínez-Hernández JC, Ramírez-Soto AF, Sheseña-Hernández I, Lucio-Palacio CR, Ruelas Inzunza E (2017) Capacity building to advance the United Nations sustainable development goals: An overview of tools and approaches related to sustainable land management. J Sustain for 37(2):157–177

Boyer E, Kolpakov A (2018) An empirical examination of partnership frequency and design within international non-governmental organisations (INGOs). Int J Public Adm 41(11):909–920

Davis JM (2019) Real "non-governmental" aid and poverty: Comparing privately and publicly financed NGOs in Canada. Canadian Journal of Development Studies/revue Canadienne D'études Du Développement 40(3):1–18

Egger C (2018) Just part-time lovers? Competition, coercive coordination, and friendship among international INGOs. Camb Rev Int Aff 30(4):394–414

Fiddian-Qasmiyeh E, Pacitto J (2019) Southern-led faith-based responses to refugees: Insights for the Global North. Religion and European Society, A Primer, pp 195–214

Ika LA, Donnelly J (2017) Success conditions for international development capacity building projects. Int J Project Manage 35(1):44–63

Lassa JA (2019) *Roles of non-government organisations in disaster risk reduction.* Oxford Research Encyclopedia of Natural Hazard Science

Martinez DE, Cooper DJ (2017) Assembling international development: Accountability and the disarticulation of a social movement. Acc Organ Soc 63:6–20

Olawoore B, Kamruzzaman P (2019) NGOs, partnership and accountability–A case study of action aid and its local NGO partners in Nigeria. In Forum for development studies 46(3): 451–471, Routledge

Oliver-Smith A (2019) Disasters and large-scale population dislocations: International and national responses. Oxford Research Encyclopedia of Natural Hazard Science

Saleh FIM, Karia N (2020) Management for international development and aid projects: A new conceptual model. Nonprofit Manag Leadersh 31(2):373–386

Saleh, FI, Karia N (2022) Adaptive project management model for the international development and aid projects. Nonprofit Management and Leadership

Sweis RJ, Saleh FIM, Dahiyat SE, Sweis NJ, Saleh RA, Diab H (2016) Benchmarking of TQM practices in INGOs: A literature review. Benchmarking: Int J 23(1): 236–261

Chapter 7
Management of Monitoring, Evaluation, Accountability, and Learning

7.1 Introduction

INGOs undertake IDAPs to operationalize their strategic objectives and add value to the lives of targeted people and communities. Therefore, they transcend the borders of their origins and operate abroad to mediate the role between international supporters and people in less developed or crises-affected countries (Kraft and Smith 2019) for the purpose of responding to humanitarian crises, promoting the socio-economic situations of people, or for post-disaster recovery and rehabilitation (Ott and Valero 2017).

Due to their position as liaisons between international donors and domestic stakeholders, INGOs are always in a position that requires them to be the most accountable to all stakeholders (Latif and Williams 2017). Therefore, they are obligated to and expected to maintain all directions of accountability when implementing their projects (Berghmans et al. 2017). These include, but are not limited to, upward accountability toward those who "give," downward accountability toward those who "receive," and horizontal accountability toward governments, partners, and communities. Likewise, they are required to maintain efficiency, which is sought by donors, and effectiveness, which is also sought by recipients of services, and in turn, they are meant to satisfy the expectations of all stakeholders in their projects that are vital to the lives of vulnerable people.

Given the aforementioned considerations, IDAPs must ensure the responsible implementation and delivery of intended support. Furthermore, they must ensure a continuous learning and adaptation process to address emerging realities, unintended or negative outcomes, and meet the changing needs and expectations of targeted people and communities. To this end, IDAPs should be monitored and evaluated, and the voices of targeted people should be taken into account to ensure the highest quality of implementation and results, accountability of funds from donors, and to inform future program design and strategies. The IDAPs' industrial functions, known

F. I. Mahmoud Saleh and N. Karia, *Value-driven Management for International Development and Aid Projects*, https://doi.org/10.1007/978-981-97-3666-9_7

as monitoring, evaluation, accountability, and learning (MEAL), should be well documented and agreed upon as IDAP's customized MEAL framework or system. This chapter discusses these four essential functions as well as their manifestations in the life cycles of IDAPs.

The sections of this chapter, therefore, are organized as follows: Sect. 7.2 discusses monitoring, including aims, data points, procedures, and modalities; Next, Sect. 7.3 explores the different types of evaluations, aims and scopes, data points, and procedures. Then, Sect. 7.4 highlights accountability to people of concern along with its key success factors. Section 7.5, however, uncovers learning, its governance, and its role and responsibilities. Lastly, Sect. 7.6 puts it all together to explain how monitoring, evaluation, accountability, and learning can be operationalized throughout the life cycle of IDAPs, i.e., PM processes for MEAL functions.

7.2 Monitoring

Monitoring works as an integral part of the overall functions of evaluation, learning, information management, and accountability to targeted people. However, it can be defined as the routine and systematic monitoring of program activities and outputs. In its essence, monitoring is the assessment of compliance and deviation from agreed-upon plans and procedures to identify and communicate the required adaptations in the current and future IDAPs. Therefore, to identify and undertake the required adaptations. Accordingly, the aggregated MEAL master plans and data collection tools will be developed and regularly updated.

The holistic monitoring approach should start with ensuring accountable targeting and selection of targeted people or entities. Therefore, MEAL departments or teams verify the eligibility and correctness of the selected program participants. Then, monitor the implementation of activities through spot-checking and observations, and conduct post-delivery assessments. Accordingly, the general procedures for IDAPs monitoring can be as follows:

- Develop and update IDAP's monitoring plans during the project's initiation phase and according to the industrial standards or broader global standards of implementing INGO to identify necessary data collection tools, reviews and assessments, disaggregation, timelines, and accountability for tracking IDAP's performance indicators.
- Conduct the contractual baseline assessments in the initial phase of IDAP's duration. Further, to technically oversee any other assessments required to be conducted for the specific requirements of the projects in coordination with the project manager or PMO.
- Contribute to project kick-off meetings to ensure that the project team, the M&E team, and senior management understand the M&E requirements, IDAP's indicators, logframe, and M&E deliverables.

- Conduct regular field observations, rapid evaluations, and data quality checks for project activities and implementing partners.
- Maintain project activity databases and data visualization tools, and ensure that IDAP's information management system(s) are updated regularly.
- Disseminate information to facilitate decision-making and timely adaptations.
- Upload all project documents to the online folders and repositories for implementing INGO, ensuring that all means of verification and relevant documentation are updated and uploaded, so as to maintain the organizational memory and facilitate access to INGO's staff of other IDAPs to any piece of information required.
- Organize regular M&E meetings with IDAP's management teams to plan M&E activities, discuss progress and findings from regular M&E activities, and produce recommendations for improvements accordingly.
- In coordination with the IDAP's managers, organize the mid-term and post-project reflections, reviews, and learning sessions to document learning that drives project adaptations.
- Undertake an after-action monitoring process to ensure decision-making effectiveness and quality of the corrected and preventive actions taken.
- Include the M&E findings for various internal and external channels, including donors' reporting, reports of implementing partners, and consultants' reports.
- Collect the required information for learning and accountability.
- Refer any feedback or complaint that emerged from the consultations with the targeted groups according to the community feedback mechanisms.

To that end, we suggest three data points that should be the focus of the monitoring function. They are:

1. Monitoring beneficiary/participant selection.
2. Activity spot-checking or monitoring of implementation.
3. Post-delivery monitoring.

For each of these three data points, there are three questions: What to monitor? How to monitor? And who to monitor? All of these should be addressed. The following example (Table 7.1) shows how these questions should be answered for each activity under IDAP.

7.3 Evaluation

Evaluation involves the periodic assessment and analysis of ongoing or completed projects and programs to identify what is working well and what needs to be improved. It should be an integral element of IDAP's learning agenda and adaptive management. Evaluation can take multiple shapes and forms depending on its purpose and timing in the IDAP's lifecycle. For example, as introduced in Chapter 4, long-term IDAPs should include mid-line, annual surveys, and end-line evaluations.

Table 7.1 Example for activity monitoring and spot-checking

Activity	Role of MEAL in targeting and selection of program participants	Role of MEAL during implementation	Role of MEAL in post-delivery monitoring
Vocational Training (VT) for Employment Purposes	Targeted groups' mobilization was primarily done through social media, contact center, and external referrals, followed by in-depth interviews with the potential program participants. Therefore, the following monitoring and activity spot-checking will take place in the selection phase to ensure eligibility, inclusion, and overall accountability of this activity: **WHAT?** • Eligibility • Inclusion **How?** • Approve the list of selected program participants for each training, to take a representative sample and validate their eligibility. This entails requesting documents and proof of eligibility • Membership of M&E team in any selection committee (when applicable) • Handle any feedback or complaints about accessing the VTs **WHO?** • M&E Officer • Adherence to SOPs of feedback and complaints mechanisms	**WHAT?** • Satisfaction • Attendance rates and actual attendees compared to attendance sheets • Verification of received amount of cash allowances based on the attendance sheet • Safety and security, fraud, safeguarding, and health risks • Gender sensitivity • Staff and trainers' attitudes • Inclusion and accessibility aspects • The overall quality of trainings • Adherence to relevant SOPs • Handle any feedback/complaint concerning the implementation of VTs **How?** • Pre/post assessments in collaboration with the trainers • field visit—three visits for each training • Approval of payment lists • M&E team to join 30% of the monitoring visits of the business owners • Membership of the relevant kits procurement committees concerning VTs **WHO?** • M&E Officer • Adherence to SOPs of feedback and complaints mechanisms	**WHAT?** • Attendance • Satisfaction • Relevancy • Effectiveness • Efficiency • Output and outcome level indicators of IDAP • Improvements needed • Awareness of feedback and complaints channels • Risks of harassment and fraud • Gender responsiveness • Inclusion and accessibility aspects • The overall quality of capacity-building activities • Adherence to relevant technical and managerial SOPs **How?** • Pre/post assessments in collaboration with the trainers • Trainers' and mentors' reports • Participants Survey, FGDs, and KII (QUAN/QUAL)—scientific and gender-disaggregated sampling design one month after receiving the kits (in case of VT for entrepreneurship and two months after VT for employment) **WHO?** • M&E Officer • Adherence to SOPs of feedback and complaints mechanisms

Complex IDAPs may need to include specific or thematic evaluations to inform implementation strategies or open-ended outcome harvesting evaluations to examine any unintended or negative impacts. INGOs that have provided funds after the end of an IDAP can also conduct ex-post evaluations of their IDAPs and broader programs to assess the long-term effects of these programs.

7.3.1 Technical Considerations and Cross-Cutting Aspects

No matter what the goal of the assessment is, it should be undertaken rigorously as it pertains to the accountability of INGOs to their stakeholders and those they are trying to help. For instance, it should be based on reliable starting points and adhere to scientific methods that lead to accurate results. Therefore, we recommend the following technical aspects be taken into account, no matter what the aim of the evaluation or methodology is:

- **Inclusion**: Inclusion is a process that ensures that those at risk of poverty and social exclusion gain the opportunities and resources necessary to participate fully in economic, social, political, and cultural life and to enjoy a standard of living that is considered normal in the society in which they live. It ensures that they have greater participation. IDAPs should be committed to ensuring the inclusion of women, youth, and persons with disabilities throughout all project interventions. This entails thoughtful and targeted planning to work around barriers that hinder their true participation. The IDAP should work to address barriers that hinder their meaningful participation in the market or social systems. The evaluation, therefore, should apply inclusion lenses to examine each data point specified as being addressed by the evaluation. Similarly, it should adhere to any relevant inclusion guiding frameworks and ensure sensitive data collection, analysis, reporting, quality assurance protocols, ethical considerations, and training of enumerators. Some organizations, however, undertake gender and age analysis, inclusion analysis, or apply gender or inclusion markers separately from the IDAP's lifecycle in order to cover multiple IDAPs. While this strategy can be an efficient one, it still needs to be undertaken carefully to ensure that it is deep enough to cover the specific activities of each IDAP.
- **System thinking**: As we discussed in Chapter 5, the assessments of the needs and opportunities of targeted people or entities should look at agency, relations, and structure levels. Therefore, IDAPs should acknowledge the positive role of well-functioning and effective markets or social systems in enhancing the situation of targeted people or the performance of targeted entities, reducing poverty, and bringing a lasting impact on the lives of people. The assessments and evaluations should consider the relevant and standard schematic of sectoral market systems, analytical frameworks, or standard value chains for inclusion or integration in the overall methodology. The datasets of evaluation, therefore, should be further reviewed, sampled and collected, analyzed, and reported based on the

role or position of targeted people or entities in the broader systems, or based on standard dimensions of relevant analytical frameworks or system maps whenever applicable.

- **Triangulation**: Regardless of the sequence or methodological approach adopted, emergent primary quantitative and qualitative findings from the various data sources should be triangulated and synthesized to emphasize contrasts and similarities when appropriate. Furthermore, the surveys and assessment should provide a comparison of the key findings that emerged with any relevant benchmarks when feasible.
- **Intersectionality and correlations**: This is to understand how aspects of the identities of targeted people or entities combine and/or correlate to create different modes of vulnerabilities or opportunities. Similarly, there are significant correlations among the identified data points. Examples of these aspects include sex, disability, sector/sub-sector, segments, governorate, and the status and age of program participants.

7.3.2 Data Points

Each evaluation has its own objectives and, in turn, data points that need to be measured accordingly. As such, the data points should be guided by a ToC, results frameworks, and implementation strategies. Similarly, the nature of each IDAP, targeted sectors, technical areas, and implementation strategies should all be considered while conducting evaluations. For instance, the evaluation of an IDAP that responds directly to fleeing refugees by providing basic needs differs from the evaluation of a five-year development project that aims to improve the agriculture market systems by collaborating with market system actors to develop new business models and enhance economic infrastructures and policies.

Through this section, we will first outline some proposed data points that can be evaluated for direct interventions, then present the ones that can be assessed for the MSD system-level intervention as an example of system-level interventions. However, these data points should consider the current stage of IDAP. For instance, they should be customized differently to fit mid-line, endline, thematic, or outcome harvesting evaluations.

Data points for the evaluation of direct interventions:

- What was the progress achieved? And/or to what extent were the project's goals, objectives, and indicators achieved?
- What works well?
- What needs to be improved, and what are the required corrective actions?
- What are the challenges and risks?
- To what extent was the project successful in identifying, analyzing, and responding to the project's risks and challenges?

- What are the preventive actions and mitigation actions required to ensure successful project completion?
- Are the planned objectives, project indicators, activities, and targets still relevant or need to be adjusted?
- What were the main factors that influenced the achievement of the project's goals and objectives?
- What is the alignment progress with INGO's global indicators and national plans?
- To what extent was the project coordinated and complemented by the rest of other IDAPs or other interventions, programs, and inter-agency responses in the context of operations, governmental strategies and plans, and all relevant stakeholders?
- What is the progress toward addressing climate change and/or negative environmental risks?
- What is the extent of targeted people's participation and inclusion in the project design, planning, and implementation?
- What is the progress toward the planned gender sensitivity scale?
- What is the extent of participation of impact groups in feedback and complaint mechanisms, and what is their ability to report % of feedback from women and girls?
- What is the extent of safeguarding and protection from sexual exploitation and abuse in the project's activities?
- To what extent was the project engaged and included the targeted people in the project design, planning, implementation, and evaluation?
- What is the extent of indirect implementation and community leadership of project activities?
- To what extent did the project's partnerships succeed in terms of satisfaction, capacity, engagement and integration, and achievement of the project's objectives?
- What is the progress of coordination and complementation in implementing the project?
- What are the progress and actions taken toward pathways to scale?
- What are the adaptations made to the project activities based on solid decision-making and the voice of targeted people?
- What is the extent of the efficiency and effectiveness of activity monitoring and spot-checking?
- To what extent were the adopted approaches to project implementation efficient?
- To what extent were internal MEAL mechanisms successful?
- What were the key challenges, lessons learned, and recommendations (including the perception of targeted people) for future programming?
- What are the top key stories of change brought about by the project in people's lives?
- What is the progress toward budget utilization rate and value for money?

Data points for evaluation of market system-level interventions:
In addition to the proposed data points mentioned above, the following data points can be considered for the market system-level evaluations; these examples are borrowed from Nippard et al. (2014) and Downing et al. (2018):

- **ADOPT**: The extent of uptake, institutionalization, and internalization of the intervention by the system actor or player, including the existence of concrete plans to continue it in the future.
- **ADAPT**: How the introduced business model(s) or investment(s) are accepted by market system actors or players, including the extent of the system actor or player's initial investment in the change (or introduced business model) independently of IDAP's support.
- **EXPAND**: To what extent have the piloted business models (or interventions) by IDAP's been replicated or multiplied by other (competing) system actors or added diversity by offering variance among them? Including the mainstreaming of business models in the market systems.
- **RESPOND**: To what extent have system actors or players reacted to and accommodated the presence of changes in market systems or behavioral changes? Including the pattern of change in supportive roles in response to behavioral changes.
- **CONNECTIVITY**: To what extent do system actors and MSEs in the market system have an optimal number of vertical and horizontal connections that ensure redundancy and mitigate the risk of sudden stopping, but do not affect innovation in the market negatively?
- **DIVERSITY**: To what extent is the system optimally diverse in terms of products, markets, market channels, and size of businesses?
- **POWER DYNAMICS**: To what extent is the exercise of power shared in the market system, and in turn, to what extent are solutions and resources distributed enough to address shocks?
- **COOPERATION**: The extent of market system actors' collaboration to add value and achieve common purposes for the interest of market system performance.
- **COMPETITION AND BUSINESS STRATEGY**: To what extent do the system actors compete on adding value and, in turn, have value-driven strategies and operational decisions?
- **EVIDENCE-BASED DECISION-MAKING**: To what extent are the system actors taking evidence-based, and in turn, less risky, decisions?
- **INCLUSIVENESS**: To what extent is the market system socially inclusive for the different genders and age groups as well as Persons Living with Disabilities (PLWD)? Including the extent of benefiting from the characteristics of specific groups (such as the innovation competencies of youth) for the interest of market system resilience.

7.3.3 Administrative Procedures for Evaluations

The evaluation process of IDAPs is heavily influenced by the nature and scope of the evaluation. However, we recommend the following general steps and considerations for project-based evaluations:

1. **Form the reference group for the evaluation**: The members of project-based evaluations should consist of, but not be limited to, the MEAL head, the program/ project director or manager, and the relevant technical leads. The role of the reference group is to guide the overall evaluation process from the beginning to the end, including providing technical inputs and revisions for all deliverables.
2. **Develop the terms of reference (TOR) and methodology of the evaluation**: The TOR is to be developed by the MEAL head of focal point, reviewed by the reference group, and approved by the head of mission.
3. **Select and meet the consultant(s) [If applicable]**: The technical committee of any evaluation should include the project manager and MEAL head. The selection process should consist of interviews with the shortlisted candidates to confirm the ability of the consultants and their understanding of the assignment.
4. **Undertake the evaluation**: The MEAL head and team should provide technical supervision to the consultancy as well as accompany the evaluation process in order to ensure the following of the agreed-upon objectives, methodology, and standards, but not to affect the independence of the evaluation.
5. **Revision of deliverables**: To be done by the reference group.
6. **Presentation and dissemination of findings**: The findings of the evaluation should be presented and submitted to the relevant stakeholders as one of the project's deliverables. The findings should also be presented to the partners (if applicable) as well as to the targeted people in order to get their feedback and concerns.
7. **Sign-off**: The sign-off on the deliverables of project-based evaluations is to be provided by the MEAL head, program/project manager, and head of mission.

7.4 Accountability to People of Concern

In a study by Fox (2018), it was emphasized that when discussing public accountability terms like right-to-know, transparency, and advocacy, it is crucial to effectively communicate these concepts to local communities. Additionally, it is important to tailor these terms in a manner that is sensitive to the domestic cultures. Likewise, building trust with the communities should be the initial priority, which can be achieved by actively listening to their voices, learning from their experiences, respecting their cultural values and religious beliefs, involving stakeholders in decision-making processes, committing to a long-term presence, adopting sustainable projects that are ultimately owned by the community, and ensuring transparency (Jamal and Baldwin 2019).

In order to institutionalize participation and a community-based approach within the implementing INGOs, it is essential to include all parts of the targeted communities rather than adopting an ad-hoc or project-based approach that may be superficial, as advocated by AbouAssi and Trent (2013). Scholars have suggested various modalities of participation that have been adopted by practitioners. These include early consultations with communities to involve them in the design of IDAPs, active engagement of communities in the implementation process, post-implementation consultations, and sharing honest and timely information with communities (Opdyke et al. 2018). It is also important to provide safe, formal, and accessible feedback and accountability mechanisms to ensure effective community participation and involvement (Sweis et al. 2016). Additionally, another significant modality is the inclusion of "community representatives," who work closely with the project team to plan and tailor projects based on their recommendations (Davis and Garb 2019). Not to mention that all implementing IGNOs should adhere to the Core Humanitarian Standards (CHS 2014). More specifically, CHS commitment four: "Communities and people affected by crises know their rights and entitlements, have access to information, and participate in decisions that affect them," and CHS commitment five: "Communities and people affected by crises have access to safe and responsive mechanisms to handle complaints." Effective feedback and complaint mechanisms are central to this commitment and to the duty of implementing INGO to prevent sexual exploitation and abuse. Accordingly, we provide in the section the following determinations before demonstrating how these determinants can be operationalized and reflected in the IDAPs life cycle:

- Importance of the feedback and complaint mechanisms.
- Key definitions.
- Feedback channels.

Importance of the feedback and complaint mechanisms

- To enhance accountability, transparency, and credibility among all stakeholders.
- To provide the targeted communities with a safe and transparent mechanism to provide their feedback, suggestions, and complaints.
- To learn from program participants, communities, and all stakeholders and be responsive to their views, opinions, and complaints to improve the quality and impact of work.
- To inform the learning and adaptive management processes and efforts.
- To meet the emerging community needs and priorities.
- To protect the safety and dignity of those who make a complaint, as well as those who are complained about, and to provide a non-judicial but respectful means for addressing grievances and the provision of redress where it is required.
- To identify potential issues and risks through an early warning system and address them in a timely manner.
- To support field staff to effectively manage feedback and complaints and to respond appropriately to less serious and more serious complaints, that can otherwise put certain staff under a great deal of stress.

Key Definitions

A Feedback and Complaint Mechanism: is a set of procedures and tools formally established (ideally across programs and linked to other monitoring processes) that:

- Solicit, collate, and analyze feedback from members of the community where INGO operates (including through partners), about their experience with the activities of IDAPs and their partners.
- Solicit, collate, and analyze feedback and complaints from partners and other stakeholders about their experience of working with the IDAP and implementing INGO.
- Trigger an action, influence the decision-making at the appropriate level in the organization, and/or prompt a referral to other relevant stakeholders if necessary and appropriate.
- Provide a response back to the person who raised the feedback (when not anonymous) and also respond to the wider community.

Feedback channels: are the platforms that people can use to communicate their feedback. The feedback and complaint mechanism should provide different channels to promote access for all community members, including people with specific needs and children.

Feedback: is a positive or negative statement, concern, or suggestion provided to the implementing INGO or partners regarding the IDAP's activities or the behavior of staff, volunteers, or representatives that allows recipients to express their concerns or displeasure.

Complaint: is a specific grievance from anyone who is dissatisfied with IDAP's activities or the behavior of staff or representatives, or who believes that implementing INGO or its partners has failed to meet a stated commitment or expected standards of behavior. Complaints can be about non-sensitive or sensitive issues such as sexual exploitation and abuse, breach of the code of conduct, corruption, extortion, fraud, or any illegal practice. A complaint allows recipients to confidentially report corruption or abuse of power and to seek redress. A complaint may be formal or informal, written or verbal, signed or anonymous.

Confidentiality: refers to the sensitive and appropriate treatment of information. Ensuring that feedback is handled in a confidential manner increases the trust people place in the system and protects them from potential harm.

Feedback Channels

Feedback channels can be static, in which individuals take the initiative to raise their feedback, and are typically preferred by individuals who wish to remain anonymous or who wish to raise sensitive concerns; these channels are always open and reachable to a wide audience, which individuals can access whenever they choose. Examples of static channels include feedback and complaint or suggestion boxes, hotlines or helplines, SMS, social media channels, and email.

Feedback channels can also be active, which means relying on the direct solicitation of community feedback through direct interactions with community members. This includes the implementation of IDAPs activities as well as the different types of data collection and consultations.

In Sect. 7.6, we provide the specific processes required to operationalize accountability to targeted people, along with the rest of MEAL functions.

7.5 Learning

The continuously changing nature of the INGOs industry, contexts of operations, as well as the continuously changing needs and priorities of targeted people, impose IDAPs on continuous learning to constantly improve implementation, adapt to meet these changes, innovate, and collaborate to share knowledge in order to achieve their ultimate objectives (Sweis et al. 2016).

USAID's ADS 200 defines learning as a continuous process of analyzing a wide variety of information sources and knowledge in order to facilitate iterative adaptation of strategy, project design, and/or implementation for more effective and efficient achievement of development objectives.

Learning forms the fundamental core and level of excellence of M&E; without learning, M&E can be a harmful effort to the targeted people. Likewise, the efficiency of using allocated resources for IDAPs. However, this aim encounters several organizational and cultural challenges. This includes, but is not limited to, a lack of resources, a lack of enabling environment, a lack of senior management commitment, and a lack of flexible program design and contractual obligations, which makes learning and adaptive management one of the key shortcomings that nag IDAPs managers and donors alike, as well as limiting the benefit of the collected data for activity monitoring and evaluation. Most of the international development donors and major INGOs, therefore, tried to impose learning frameworks and do learning and adapt programs deliberately through allocating resources and managerial structures to operationalize learning within and among IDAPs.

In its essence, this book reflects the convergence of relevant IDAPs' management theories with the practical issues and field experience of the authors. The management literature is full of evidence on the importance of learning to continuous improvement in organizational excellence, overall performance, and the impact of businesses. Therefore, we focus through the next sections on the practical manifestations of learning in the IDAPs and, in turn, in the INGOs industry as a whole.

7.5.1 Learning Agenda

Commitment to learning should be manifested in the form of a clear learning agenda, systematic learning processes, dedicated resources, intentional "pause and reflect" moments, and commitment to adapt: these are the things that should be well articulated in the IDAP's learning plan(s) or agenda(s). In essence, the learning plan or agenda aims to identify the areas that the IDAP and its programmatic components intentionally and explicitly want to learn about to build knowledge and improve programming. This is to prove or disprove the assumptions and causal relationships of ToC, shape assessments and evaluations, improve implementation, inform strategic alignments, and contribute to the broader learning agenda of the implementing INGOs or confederation.

While the learning agenda is a live document that should be regularly updated with the continuously emerging learning questions, it can be drafted with the initially identified learning questions according to the programmatic components of the main interventions and then elaborated and updated as the implementation goes. As such, the identified questions should be narrowed down and scheduled based on the availability of resources and strategic priorities of the IDAP and implementing INGO. However, smart IDAPs' managers and INGOs' leaders should make sure to allocate the required resources to put the planned learning agenda into action; this includes assigning clear roles and responsibilities as well as assigning budget lines to apply the emerged and agreed-upon adaptations. Therefore, to enforce learning as well as to avoid any contractual budget or scope constraints, one must apply these adaptations.

7.5.2 Learning Process

Despite the variety of learning frameworks adopted by the different major INGOs in the world, it can be said that learning processes can be summarized into the following six general cyclic steps, as shown in Fig. 7.1.

Learning should begin by interacting with IDAP's important internal and external stakeholders to identify learnings and their potential sources. Internal stakeholders can include the relevant technical leads who design activities and identify the implementation modalities and those who are implementing the activities of IDAP on the ground, focusing on front liners because of their direct interaction with targeted people. It is also required to work closely with the M&E teams and research teams if they operate as separate entities. The external stakeholders, however, can include other peer organizations and IDAPs, particularly those who have similar or intersecting mandates. External stakeholders can also include research institutes,

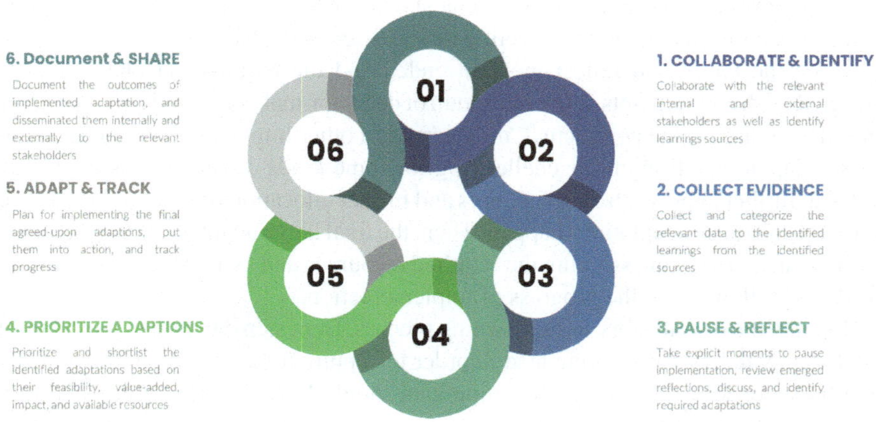

Fig. 7.1 General learning process

academics, and research centers, as well as any relevant stakeholders to the objectives of IDAP and its interventions. This step includes the identification of relevant global institutes or organizations that publish best practices and standards applicable to work approaches and implementation modalities adopted by the IDAP.

The main aims of this collaboration are to identify learning sources and questions concerning the learning agenda of IDAP and then agree on co-planning to collect the required data with those stakeholders.

Once the co-plans are established, the secondary data and primary data collection of evidence should take place accordingly. The secondary data can be pushed as agreed with their producers or pulled from their sources as identified in the previous step and according to the established plans. However, the primary data can be collected using regular data collection, such as M&E data collection and ongoing research. It can also be done specifically and separately by the learning personnel. Likewise, it can be shared by the front-liners and implementation teams.

Guided by the learning agenda and implementation plans, the learning personnel and IDAP's leaders should be able to determine suitable moments of pause and reflection. Typically, these moments arise as decision gates between activities or phases to discuss the effectiveness, efficacy, and overall quality of work done before moving forward to the next activity or phase. Likewise, it can be during implementation. It can also be done by bringing the relevant stakeholders to large gatherings or workshops or by small groups of implementers.

As part of these sessions and discussions, the learning personnel or organizers should start by presenting recommendations, lessons learned, and proposed adaptations. Regardless of the size or timing of pause and reflect moments, the learning personnel who organize these moments should follow the best practices of communications, meetings, and workshops by bringing the right people to the table and ensuring effective discussions and safe spaces to contribute to these discussions, while also making sure that the participants come to the discussion after reading the relevant learning brief. However, the outcome of pause and reflect moments should be in the form of a list of adaptations that should move forward in the process; this can be done through anonymous voting on the discussed adaptations.

Once the pause and reflect moment ended and the required adaptations were selected by the participants, a smaller group of decision-makers should come together in order to discuss the contractual, monetary, and other implications of undertaking these adaptations. It might be challenging for some kinds of agreements to change without further approval from the donors and further allocations of resources to move forward and make adaptations happen. Then, the final list of adaptations will be in the form of an action plan assigning the required resources and ownership. The learning lead is to follow up on the progress of implementation.

Finally, the overall story of the learning process, from step one to step five, should be documented by the learning lead in order to capture the emerging improvements and their impacts. As such, the learning lead should have the storytelling capacity to showcase and articulate the cycle of improvement through readable and publishable documentation as well as presentations focusing on telling the story of IDAP's program participants, including how they were affected by the improvement achieved and what the added value is for them. This is to disseminate them internally and externally. These actions can be considered the closure of the feedback loop and should include an appreciation of those who participate and support the overall learning process by motivating them to generate further improvement suggestions. Smart leaders should make sure to incorporate learning into the objectives and performance appraisal processes of their staff to ensure that learning is part of the staff's responsibilities and to govern the learning culture, which will be discussed further in the next section (Sweis et al. 2016).

7.5.3 Learning Culture

A supportive culture is the oil of the learning machine, which should touch every part of it; without it, learning processes will not be realized. Each step of the learning process should be associated with the attention of IDAP's leaders, and learning leads to cultural aspects. For instance, collaboration and co-planning should be preceded by introductory communications to ensure that both internal and external stakeholders are fully aware of the importance of learning and continuous improvement to their scopes of work, to the overall excellence of their organizations, projects, and areas of work, and ultimately to positively impact the situation of targeted people and communities.

It is well known among academics and practitioners alike that a learning-supportive culture starts from the CEO's room and senior leadership team to be a role model for learning and adaptive management, and by ensuring the availability and support of safe, inclusive, and diverse spaces for all to learn.

As the author of this book, I used to ensure that any induction program or meeting with any newly joined staff should include a piece of orientation on the importance of learning and emphasize openness to any new ideas, especially those coming from the implementing INGO as external eyes. Therefore, to challenge the status quo where applicable, I am keen to keep a tablet on my desk with the following quote as well:

> People who are crazy enough to think they can change the world are the ones who do.—Rob Siltanen

This should be a constant organizational message across IDAP that should be conveyed by the supervisors at all levels whenever possible when communicating with the team members. It also should be operationalized by incorporating the extent of participation in improvement suggestions, adaptation, and innovation as part of the appraisal and performance management systems which incentivize and reward improvement suggestions and adaptations.

Pause and reflect exercises should not only be dealt with as a step of the learning process but also as a norm and tradition of the field staff as a regular practice to inform the decisions between implementation steps and activities.

7.5.4 Knowledge Management System

In order to govern and operationalize the learning process and to document and communicate learning, the IDAP should establish and adopt a tailored knowledge management system and platform. In this book, we suggest an adapted version of the Knowledge Management Cycle, which has been adopted by various international development actors, including USAID, UNDP, and CARE. The rest of this section presents the proposed KMC's stages as follows:

1. **Knowledge Generation:** Knowledge can be generated in the IDAP from several sources. Such as, but not limited to, monthly monitoring reports, regular and ad-hoc evaluations, and reviews, needs assessments, accountability spot-checks, regular feedback and complaint reports, outreach activities, meeting minutes, M&E meetings and staff reflections, reception surveys, coordination working group meetings with other development actors in the areas of operation, as well as assessments of peer organizations.

   The knowledge management system should identify the roles and responsibilities as well as time frames for generating intended knowledge that should mostly be guided by the learning agenda of the IDAP and implementing INGO.
2. **Knowledge Capture, Organization, and Sharing:** This stage entails capturing, organizing, and documenting the collected learnings to be accessible and ready to be used for decision-making. To that end, data analytics and visualization are irreplaceable.

   The knowledge management system should ensure the assignment of required resources to upload learnings and visualize them to have the best readable formats for targeted audiences and decision-makers.
3. **Knowledge Adaptation and Use:** This stage aims to reflect the knowledge and use it for projects and program adaptations, multiplying impact, and forthcoming intervention and activity designs. A champion should be assigned to undertake and follow up on each learning and, in turn, adaptation as identified in the learning process.

7.6 Project Management Processes for MEAL

In this chapter, we unpacked the four essential functions of MEAL that should be dealt with as mandatory functions for ensuring the ultimate quality and accountability of the IDAPS. We concluded the chapter by providing systematic processes that can be used by the IDAPs leaders to ensure that these essential functions are undertaken as an integral part of the overall project management processes as proposed by Saleh and Karia (2022). While we stress the collective responsibility of the management team in ensuring the quality and accountability in IDAP by considering the MEAL functions as part of IDAP's life cycle, this integration should not affect the assumed independence of MEAL as an accountability tool for IDAP.

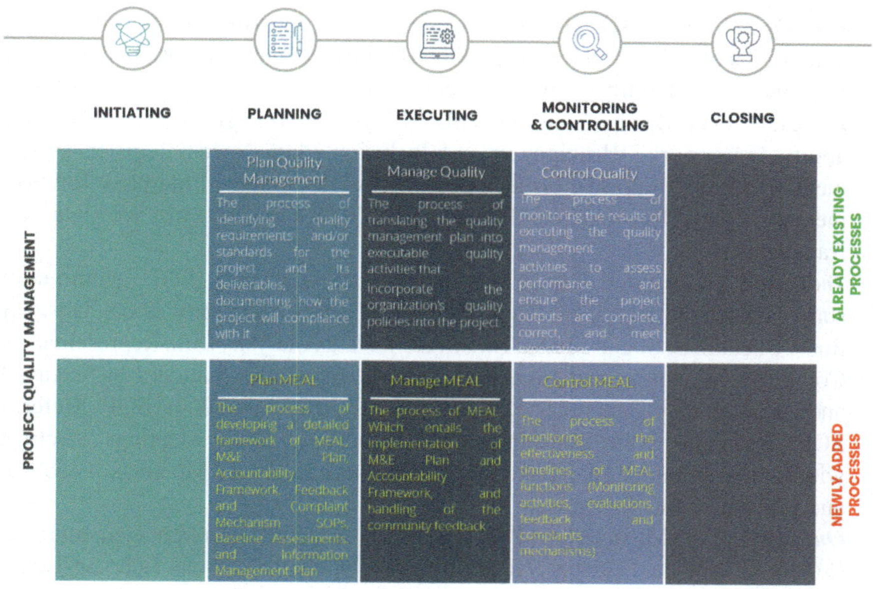

Fig. 7.2 Project management processes for MEAL functions

In their project management model for IDAPs, Saleh and Karia (2022) outlined three interlinked processes for MEAL functions as follows (see Fig. 7.2):

Process 1: Plan MEAL. The process of developing a detailed framework of MEAL, M&E Plan, Accountability Framework, Feedback and Complaint Mechanism SOPs, and Baseline Assessments.

Inputs: Project Charter, Project Management Plan, Agreements, Project Documents (High-Level Logframe/ToC), Enterprise Environmental Factors, Organizational Process Assets (Need Assessments, and Logframe, Strategic plan of INGO).

Tools and Techniques: Expert Judgments, Data Gathering (FGDs, community surveys, community feedback, baseline assessments, desk reviews, or primary data collection to analyze the different needs of stakeholders), Data Analysis, Data Representation, Interpersonal and Team Skills, Meetings (meetings with beneficiaries, partners, and key informants), Feedback and Complaint Mechanism, minimum standards for feedback and complaint mechanism, IASC (Protection from SEA)—Global SOPs.

Outputs: Project Management Plan Updates, Project Document Updates, MEAL Framework (Revised Logframe if needed), M&E Plan, Accountability Framework (Expected behaviors, and SOPs for the feedback and complaint mechanism), and Change Request.

Process 2. Manage MEAL. The process of managing project monitoring, evaluation, accountability, and learning. Which entails the implementation of the M&E Plan and accountability framework, and the handling of community feedback.
Inputs: Project Management Plan (MEAL Framework, MEAL Plan), Accountability Framework, Participation and Inclusion Plan, Needs Register, Agreements (Project Proposal), Project Documents (Logframe), Enterprise Environmental Factors, Organizational Process Assets (Need assessments, accountability framework).
Tools and Techniques: Expert Judgments, Data Gathering (FGDs, community surveys, and community feedback, Complaint Boxes, Electronic Tools, Observations, Checklists, Social Media, Email, etc.), Data Analysis, Data Representation, Complaints Handling and Escalation Process, Minimum Standard of Feedback and Complaint Mechanism, IASC (Protection from SEA)—Global SOPs, Referral SOPs, Real-time Evaluations, Interpersonal and Team Skills, Meetings (meetings with beneficiaries, partners, and key informants), Learning Meetings, Feedback and Complaint Mechanisms.
Outputs: Project Management Plan Updates (Communication Management Plan), Project Document Updates (Needs Register Updates, Lessons Learned Log—Knowledge Management), MEAL Findings (Monitoring Findings, Project Evaluations, Feedback and Compliant Log—*these outputs are to be inputs for the communication management processes*), Donor's and Internal Reports, Issue Log Updates), Change Requests.

Process 3: Control MEAL. The process of monitoring the effectiveness and timeliness of MEAL functions includes, but is not limited to, monitoring activities, real-time evaluations, feedback and complaint handling, and following-up on serious complaints.
Inputs: Project Management Plan (M&E Plan), Agreements (Project Proposal), Project Documents (Logframe, Accountability Framework, MEAL Framework), MEAL Findings, Escalated complaints on SEA, discrimination or any serious complaints, work performance data, enterprise environmental factors, organizational process assets (need assessments, accountability framework).
Tools and Techniques: Expert Judgments, Meetings, Feedback and Complaint Mechanism SOPs, Escalation and Investigation Techniques, Record Management, Data Gathering, Observations, Data Analysis, Data Representation, Interpersonal and Team Skills, Learning Meetings.
Outputs: Regular Accountability Reports, Success Stories, and Case Studies—*to be inputs for communications and advocacy*. Project Management Plan Updates (Communication Management Plan, HR Plan), Project Document Updates (Lessons Learned Register—Knowledge Management, Issue Log, Needs Register, Risk Register), and Learning Reports.

References

Berghmans M, Simons M, Vandenabeele J (2017) What is negotiated in negotiated accountability? The case of INGOs. Voluntas 28(4):1529–1561

Core Humanitarian Standard (CHS) (2014) Core humanitarian standard on quality and accountability. HAP International, People in Aid, and the Sphere Project, Geneva

Davis JM, Garb Y (2019) Participatory shaping of community futures in e-waste processing hubs: complexity. Conflict and stewarded convergence in a Palestinian context. Dev Policy Rev 37(1):67–89

Downing J, Field M, Ripley M, Sebstad J (2018) Market systems resilience: a framework for measurement. USAID Building Capacity for African Agricultural Transformation (Africa Lead II). https://www.resiliencelinks.org/resources/reports/market-systems-resilience-framework-measurement

Fox J (2018) The political construction of accountability keywords. IDS Bulletin 49(2)

Jamal A, Baldwin C (2019) Angels of mercy or smiling western invaders? community's perception of NGOs in northwest Pakistan. Int Soc Work 62(1):89–104

Kraft K, Smith JD (2019) Between international donors and local faith communities: Intermediaries in humanitarian assistance to Syrian refugees in Jordan and Lebanon. Disasters 43(1):24–45

Latif KF, Williams N (2017) Team effectiveness in non-governmental organisations (NGOs) projects. Eval Program Plann 64:20–32

Nippard D, Hitchins R, Elliot D (2014) Adopt-adapt-expand-respond: a framework for managing and measuring systemic change processes. The Springfield Centre. https://beamexchange.org/uploads/filer_public/4d/d3/4dd384d0-a9d6-4fb1-8da4-837968926a5d/adoptadaptexpandrespond_compressed.pdf

Opdyke A, Javernick-Will A, Koschmann M (2018) A comparative analysis of coordination, participation, and training in post-disaster shelter projects. Sustainability 10(11):4241

Ott JS, Valero JN (2017) Nongovernmental organisations and international nongovernmental organisations. Global Encyclopedia of Public Administration, Public Policy, and Governance.

Saleh FI, Karia N (2022) Adaptive project management model for the international development and aid projects. Nonprofit Management and Leadership.

Sweis RJ, Saleh FIM, Dahiyat SE, Sweis NJ, Saleh RA, Diab H (2016) Benchmarking of TQM practices in INGOs: a literature review. Benchmarking Int J 23(1):236–261

Chapter 8
Management of Advocacy and Communication with Communities

8.1 Introduction

"*For me, it is a tool that is not very useful for political advocacy where you want to promote behavioral changes,*" Martinez and Cooper (2017) quoted one of the directors of INGO when they discussed the feasibility of a logical framework as one of the traditional project management models for IDAPs. This, however, is what this book is all about, i.e., challenging traditional project management for IDAPs toward more fit-for-use and value-added project management disciplines in line with the work of Saleh and Karia (2020) and Saleh and Karia (2022). As a building block of this book, the current chapter unpacks the project management aspects relevant to managing IDAPs in terms of advocacy and communication with communities.

Responsible advocacy and communication with the targeted communities were outstanding aspects that have been addressed by most of the IDAPs' industry-specific frameworks, such as Core Humanitarian Standards (CHS) and Accountability Now. Therefore, advocacy should be wisely communicated with the local communities and should be customized as well as sensitive to the domestic cultures toward the adoption of sustainable, added-value, and eventual community-owned interventions and projects (Jamal and Baldwin 2019).

Advocacy is dealt with by practitioners as a separate technical discipline. However, the IDAPs managers have something to be aware of because of its relevance to communicating with their targeted communities and local authorities, who are key stakeholders in almost all IDAPs. Therefore, it should be under the radar of IDAP's management, specifically in terms of its strategic alignment with IDAP's objectives as well as the protection of people of concern. This call is aligned with the broad acknowledgment of literature on the importance of considering the wider social and organizational aspects of the management of IDAPs for the purpose of ensuring the sustainability and ultimate success of these projects (McEvoy et al. 2016; Steinfort 2017).

F. I. Mahmoud Saleh and N. Karia, *Value-driven Management for International Development and Aid Projects*, https://doi.org/10.1007/978-981-97-3666-9_8

In this chapter, the focus is initially placed on highlighting the significance of advocacy as an added-value effort. Subsequently, the discussion shifts toward strategizing advocacy initiatives. Following this, the chapter delves into the planning and implementation of advocacy actions, encompassing the identification of resources as well as the monitoring and evaluation of progress. The chapter concludes by exploring the intricacies of communication with communities, ethical practices in advocacy, and the interconnection between advocacy and fundraising.

8.2 Value-Added Advocacy

While advocacy is a core business of several INGOs, such as Oxfam, it has been widely acknowledged as an integral part and a vehicle for most major INGOs to realize their visions, missions, and strategic goals around the globe, such as CARE International and Mercy Corps to impact at scale and sustain the outcomes of their IDAPs. Likewise, advocacy can be undertaken on the strategic level of IDAP. Additionally, this is to influence policy change or address certain systematic barriers on the market systems level or the operational level, and to implement interventions that entail behavioral change.

CARE International defines advocacy as "*the deliberate process of influencing those who make decisions about developing, changing, and implementing policies [in CARE's case: to reduce poverty and achieve social justice]*" (CARE International 2014). As the author of this book, I worked for several INGOs that rely on advocacy as a driver to achieve their ambitious global strategic targets that aim to affect the lives of millions of people. The thing that could not be done without affecting the structural barriers and constraints in the areas of operations. In this paradigm, INGOs use advocacy to multiply impact or impact at scale through changing policies related to solving underlying causes of poverty, such as laws related to allowing women or people with specific needs to access certain services or control over certain resources.

One of the key manifestations of advocacy on the strategic level can be seen in the IDAPs that adopt market system development approaches aiming to address gaps on the market system level. Such as changing the laws related to removing legal or taxation constraints or easing governmental processes. Usually, such advocacy is integrated into implementation modalities like social accountability mechanisms or public–private dialogues.

On the operational or implementation level of advocacy, the most known form of advocacy can be noticed in the IDAPs, which aim to influence the behaviors of targeted communities. Such as targeting a certain community to change their hygiene behaviors to reduce rates of increase in communicable diseases through social media, radio, and community campaigning.

Regardless of the aim of advocacy or the level where it operates, it should be informed by evidence and work together with the communications functions in the IDAP or implementing INGO, and in turn, the IDAP's management should be aware of integrating these functions in a way that serves the successful achievements of the

IDAP's objectives and ensures quality, inclusive, ethical, and protected communications with the relevant stakeholders and communities. To that end, the value-added advocacy for the interest of IDAP's success can be summarized into the following considerations:

- **Evidence-based**: Advocacy should be grounded in reliable evidence and facts to inform decision-making and build strong cases. An irreplaceable source to inform advocacy is research. Research, however, can be done by collecting primary data specifically for the purpose of informing certain advocacy objectives, or it can be done by collecting and analyzing the existing data sets or relevant published research.
- **Linkage with MEAL functions**: MEAL functions are essential for both informing advocacy and measuring the realization of its objectives. Therefore, the emerging findings from monitoring and evaluation activities should be considered as intended or unintended sources of evidence for advocacy. The same applies to the community concerns collected through the feedback and complaint mechanisms that usually represent the verbatim voice of people of concern. As such, advocacy should be associated with the required MEAL system to monitor the progress of advocacy efforts, evaluate advocacy gains, improve, and learn from adopted advocacy modalities.
- **Linkage with stakeholder management processes**: advocacy is all about interacting with stakeholders, including those who make policy decisions, market systems actors, or program participants who are targeted by behavioral change interventions. This, however, entails project management efforts, such as but not limited to the identification of those stakeholders, analyzing their position with the IDAP in terms of power and interest, identifying their current level of engagement with the IDAP, and taking actions to meet the required level of engagement for the advocacy purposes. While these functions might be undertaken by the assigned advocacy personnel, they should be on the radar of IDAP's management team and work hand in hand with the process of IDAP's stakeholder management plans as they are directly related to the overall success or failure of IDAP.
- **Linkage with Risk Management**: Interacting with host governments and communities entails an acknowledged complexity, and in turn, the risk for IDAPs (Saleh and Karia 2020). Therefore, the risks of intermediating the role between donors' mandates and realities on the ground should be identified, analyzed, and addressed together by the advocacy team and IDAP's management team to ensure the safe achievement of IDAP's objectives.

Advocacy is neither communication nor fundraising. However, it should work closely and exchange information with the processes of communication with communities and fundraising. Therefore, to add value to the success and sustainability of IDAP alike, Sect. 8.5 unpacks these relationships accordingly.

8.3 Strategizing Advocacy

Like any successful piece of work, advocacy should be strategically aligned. In the case of IDAPs, advocacy should be most importantly aligned with the overall implementation strategy of the IDAP, with the relevant ToCs, and with the in-country or global organizational vision, mission, and strategic objectives of the implementing INGO.

Whatever the required level of strategic alignment is, advocacy should be grounded in and guided by an advocacy strategy that accumulates the organizational experience of undertaking IDAPs to address the root causes of social and economic problems beyond the directly targeted people and communities.

Advocacy management includes the formulation of an advocacy strategy, advocacy planning, advocacy implementation, and advocacy monitoring and evaluation. These functions, in fact, are interlinked. Yet they are difficult to articulate without overlapping. This section, however, highlights the key components of the advocacy strategy, while the next chapter discusses the steps for advocacy planning, implementation, monitoring, and evaluation.

Advocacy strategies can be varied based on their objectives. However, it should follow a logical format that makes it linked with the organizational vision and mission, as well as evidence-based and contextual-based. Accordingly, an advocacy strategy can include the following five sequential parts:

1. **Context**: Description of the context of concern, general social, economic, and political in-country situation, the already existing or introduced policies relevant to the IDAP's mission and objectives, and the targeted concerns as identified by the available evidence.
2. **Rationale and focus**: Narrowing down the focus of contextual analysis, advocacy priorities, and policies that are relevant to the IDAP and that have the highest potential to contribute to the objectives of the IDAP or implementing INGO. This includes identifying the specific contribution of IDAP's advocacy efforts to the overall inter-agency advocacy efforts in the areas of operation.
3. **Guiding frameworks**: Identification and establishment of the linkages between the advocacy strategy and the relevant strategies of IDAP, implementing INGO's strategy; regional strategies; inter-agency strategies; or global strategies. Furthermore, identification of any technical frameworks or standards will be adopted by advocacy efforts.
4. **Advocacy goals and objectives**: Identification of advocacy's aim and objectives, impact statement, specific description of targeted policies and intended changes, key advocacy messages, and specific description of expected breakthroughs.

8.4 Advocacy Planning and Implementation

Once the strategic goals and objectives of advocacy are identified, the advocacy efforts can be planned and operationalized. As we mentioned in the previous section, the steps of advocacy management are not easy to be segregated. However, this section focuses on the steps of planning, implementing, monitoring, and evaluating advocacy. To that end, we suggest three key steps, namely, identifying resources, action planning and implementation, and advocacy monitoring and evaluation.

8.4.1 Identify Resources

In order to plan and budget for advocacy efforts effectively, it is essential to first evaluate existing organizational capabilities and abilities to influence change, resources, and potential sources of funding to support these efforts. The existing resources can be human resources, financial resources, time, information, trust and relationships, partners to support, and networks. Then, identify potential donors or funding opportunities to finance the project at this stage. By doing these activities, it will be possible to determine the feasibility and attainability of strategic advocacy objectives and identify breakthroughs.

8.4.2 Action Planning and Implementation

Once the breakthroughs are identified and the availability as well as achievability of planned objectives are determined, the actions and activities required to realize these objectives should be placed on a time-phased and budgeted plan to be a subsidiary plan in the overall IDAP's management plan to be leveled and coordinated along with the rest of IDAP's subsidiary plans.

The first aspect that should be considered by the advocacy subject matter experts when developing the advocacy management plan is ensuring the availability of evidence to inform the different activities of advocacy. As we mentioned in Sect. 8.2, the sources of evidence can vary. The evidence can already be published by other stakeholders, collected as part of the primary data collected by IDAP's other activities and functions, or collected specifically for IDAP's advocacy efforts. Accordingly, the first kind of action on the advocacy management plan is mostly activities to gather, analyze, and visualize timely evidence.

Usually, advocacy cannot be undertaken by a single IDAP or INGO. Therefore, it should be coordinated in order to achieve its objectives with other stakeholders collectively. Therefore, coordination activities and lobbying are important candidate activities to be addressed by the advocacy management plan. Lobbying can also be used to engage the key stakeholders of concern and decision-makers by meeting and influencing them. This can also be done by arranging field visits for those stakeholders to the sites of operations.

Public campaigning is another effective modality to influence decision-makers and create political will. However, campaigning needs to be carefully planned in order to be relevant to the targeted groups, context-based, and cultural-sensitive. Nowadays, social media is one of the most important venues to be used for campaigning. However, this venue also has its specificities. For instance, Twitter might be the best choice for raising awareness in specific contexts and with certain stakeholders. Other venues might be more suitable to target certain age or gender groups, such as Instagram or Facebook.

To ensure the ultimate sustainability and community ownership, we introduced in Chapter 6 the management of the community leadership domain as a new discipline that should be expertly planned, managed, and controlled by IDAP's managers. One key relevance of adopting this domain of PM for IDAPs is the reliance on the different kinds of community structures to advance advocacy efforts. Community structures, therefore, can play a vital and irreplaceable role in facilitating and communicating advocacy messages and contributing to the identified breakthroughs.

Community structures can be in the form of community leaders or representatives, community committees, women or leadership councils, civil society networks, labor unions, or any other local actors or networks. These structures, as discussed in Chapter 6, need to be identified, trained, capacitated, and empowered to take ownership of and sustain the IDAP after the end of the IDAP. For the purposes of advocacy, however, they should be explicitly mobilized and engaged in all advocacy efforts, activities, events, and communications. Their role and presence should be dominant. The international presence, therefore, should be behind to ensure accountability, transparency, and standard communications, but not to take the role of direct interaction with the targeted audiences anyway.

8.4.3 Monitoring and Evaluation for Advocacy

M&E for advocacy is not exempt from the standard M&E functions and indicator frameworks. However, it necessitates tailoring to the specific requirements and nature of advocacy activities. For instance, it is crucial to clearly define the desired wins, breakthroughs, and impacts that the advocacy efforts aim to achieve. Additionally, M&E plans for advocacy should follow a logical approach that involves tracking short-term outputs, assessing intermediate outcomes, and evaluating the ultimate impacts of the advocacy initiatives.

To that end, we suggest in this book the following structure for a result framework aiming to link advocacy activities with its ultimate goals and, in turn, to monitor and evaluate the intermediate wins, outcomes, impacts, and contribution to the IDAP's and organizational strategic objectives: See Fig. 8.1, Advocacy Results Framework.

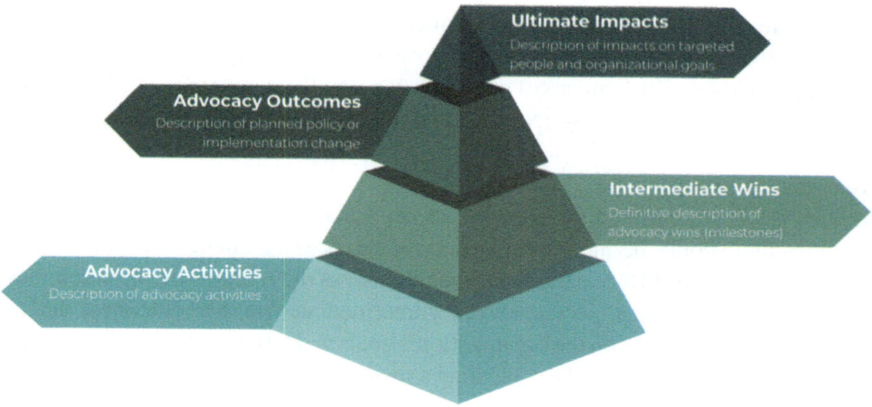

Fig. 8.1 Advocacy results framework

Ultimate Impacts

The first step in developing the advocacy results framework is to define the impact statement for IDAP's advocacy efforts. This, however, is to be done through two levels. The first level is the description of intended quantified impacts on the lives of people to be articulated in line with the overall goal and objectives of the IDAP. Then, the organizational goals will be accomplished to bring a lasting impact on the lives of the targeted people. By using this dual definition of impact, the IDAP will be able to cover both the advocacy goals of its targeted communities and the implementing organization alike.

Advocacy Outcomes

Next to the identification of the advocacy impact, the advocacy outcomes can be defined. In simple advocacy missions, this level of results framework can be skipped to the next smaller level, which comes in the form of intermediate advocacy wins. However, in the larger advocacy missions, it will be required to clearly define the intended policy and institutional changes required to realize the advocacy impact.

Intermediate Wins

Intermediate wins are the smaller intended policy and institutional changes that should be achieved collectively to realize the broader advocacy outcomes or impacts. The following examples can be considered intermediate advocacy wins:

- Influence a donor or a governmental service provider to include certain community parts or people with specific needs in their targeted populations.
- Influence a large catering services company to source their raw products from the small farmers in the local area.
- Influence a leading factory in the area of operation to adopt more restricted policies and practices for carbon dioxide emissions.
- Influence the heads of households in a targeted community to enroll their daughters in the hygiene promotion information sessions.

Regardless of what the advocacy intermediate wins or outcomes are, they should be well defined. A good definition of advocacy wins should determine reasonable timeframes for the achievements of advocacy wins. It also should include the expected role of IDAP or implementing INGO in making the intended change happen.

Advocacy Activities

In Sect. 8.4.2, we outlined the specific activities that can be classified as advocacy activities and should be incorporated into the advocacy management plan. Therefore, it is crucial for M&E leads to thoroughly assess the relationship between these proposed activities, the projected advocacy intermediate wins and outcomes, and the overall intended impacts on the organization's goals and target audience. This section underscores the importance of establishing a strong alignment and coherence between the activities and their expected outcomes, guaranteeing that the advocacy endeavors make a meaningful contribution to the desired organizational objectives and effectively benefit the intended beneficiaries. Accordingly, each expected advocacy win or outcome should include at least one or more activities.

8.5 Communication with Communities and Fundraising

In a study by Fox (2018), it was emphasized that when discussing public accountability terms like right-to-know, transparency, and advocacy, it is crucial to effectively communicate these concepts to local communities. Additionally, it is important to tailor these terms in a manner that is sensitive to domestic cultures. Similarly, building trust with the communities should be the initial priority, which can be achieved by actively listening to their voices, learning from their experiences, respecting their cultural values and religious beliefs, involving stakeholders in decision-making processes, committing to a long-term presence, adopting sustainable projects that are ultimately owned by the community, and ensuring transparency (Jamal and Baldwin 2019).

The successful implementation of advocacy necessitates close collaboration with the cross-cutting function of community communication and other outreach functions within the IDAP organizational structure. This includes activities such as campaigns and initiatives aimed at behavioral change. As a result, the advocacy function often aligns or intersects with the organizational units responsible for communications and outreach. Similarly, fundraising functions are also closely linked to advocacy, as the outcomes and achievements of advocacy efforts are frequently utilized to inform and bolster fundraising appeals. See Fig. 8.2.

Drawing from the aforementioned points, IDAP's management should be mindful of some extended considerations that aim to maximize positive risks while also mitigating negative risks when doing advocacy in collaboration with communication with communities and fundraising.

Communication with communities has been acknowledged as a key complexity for IDAPs (Saleh and Karia 2020). Therefore, communication with the public should

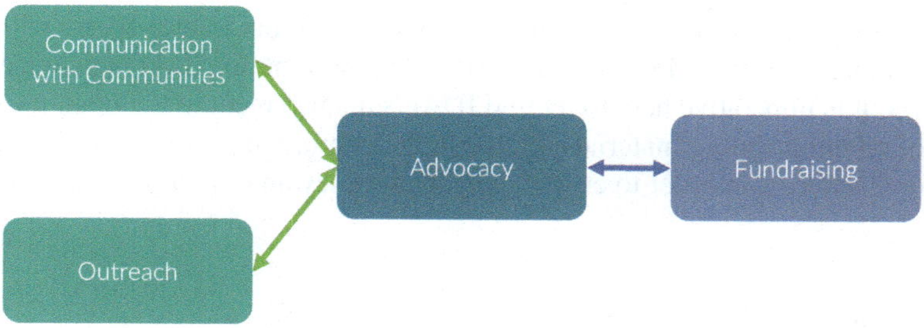

Fig. 8.2 Relationship between advocacy, communication with communities, and fundraising

be managed closely and carefully by IDAP's management. When advocacy is delivered or interacted with the public, if not undertaken wisely, it can be destructive to the overall IDAP or implementing INGO's mission. Therefore, any published material should be passed through critical revisions using local lenses without compromising the relevant values of humanitarian responses or international development standards. Therefore, the active role of local structures in revision advocacy communications is essential. Furthermore, a critical risk assessment needs to be in place to identify potential conflicts with the local government and communities before approving any advocacy-related publications or communications. Again, without compromising the superior values of IDAP or INGO.

Before implementing project activities, it is crucial to carefully analyze the cultural sensitivity of the targeted individuals, as well as their gender and age-specific information needs. This analysis should inform the selection of appropriate information channels. Various channels, such as social media, on-site leaflets, and verbal communication, should be utilized accordingly. The information shared should encompass the selection criteria for IDAP's program participants, as well as the processes and timeliness of services. All these aspects should be incorporated into the communication management plan, which will be managed and controlled throughout the communication management processes during the execution, monitoring, and controlling phases of communication with communities.

Photography and filming are widely used by practitioners to showcase and advocate for the needs of vulnerable people. However, ethical considerations must be the first priority and the key lens applied before any dissemination of the photos. IDAP's staff must obtain prior consent from the targeted individuals and provide a clear explanation of how the photos will be used. Taking photos of the targeted individuals without consent is strictly prohibited. To ensure ethical practices, it is essential to incorporate ethical considerations from relevant sector standards, INGO guidelines, and humanitarian work. These considerations are an integral part of the organizational process assets of any IDAP.

According to Saleh et al. (2017), retaining donors is considered a crucial aspect of IDAP's success. To achieve this, IDAP's management employs various strategies, such as consistently sharing advocacy outcomes, visually presenting evidence of the needs and priorities of targeted communities, and showcasing the impact of IDAP's activities on people of concern for fundraising purposes. In Chapter 10, we will delve into the management of donors as a significant discipline for IDAP's management. However, it is imperative here to remind IDAP's management to maintain the sensitivity of communicating materials related to the community, even when advocating for people's needs, in order to ensure ethical advocacy and fundraising practices.

References

CARE International (2014) The CARE international advocacy handbook. CARE International. https://www.care-international.org/files/files/Care%20International%20Advocacy%20Handbook.pdf

Fox JA (2018) The political construction of accountability keywords. IDS Bull 49(2)

Jamal A, Baldwin C (2019) Angels of mercy or smiling Western invaders? Community's perception of NGOs in Northwest Pakistan. Int Soc Work 62(1):89–104

Martinez DE, Cooper DJ (2017) Assembling international development: accountability and the disarticulation of a social movement. Acc Organ Soc (63):6–20

McEvoy P, Brady M, Munck R (2016) Capacity development through international projects: a complex adaptive systems perspective. Int J Manag Proj Bus 9(3):528–545

Saleh FIM, Karia N (2020) Management for international development and aid projects: A new conceptual model. Nonprofit Manag Leadersh 31(2):373–386

Saleh FIM, Sweis RJ, Abdelqader BY, Abdallah AB, Arafeh M (2017) The effect of TQM dimensions on the performance of international non-governmental organisations operating in Jordan. Int J Prod Qual Manage 21(4):443–459

Saleh FI, Karia N (2022) Adaptive project management model for the international development and aid projects. Nonprofit Management and Leadership.

Steinfort P (2017) Community and post-disaster program management methodology. Int J Project Manage 35(5):788–801

Chapter 9
Management of Social Workers and Resources

9.1 Introduction

The significance of Human Resources (HR) in the success of IDAPs has been widely recognized by both scholars and practitioners (Saleh et al., 2017). This acknowledgment stems not only from the importance of HR as a crucial project management discipline but also from the unique nature of these specific projects.

In the study conducted by Sweis et al. (2016), Staff Focus was identified as the fourth dimension of Total Quality Management (TQM) toward sustainability and adding value to the lives of targeted people. As a result, it is crucial for INGOs, especially front-line staff, to be empowered to address the needs and priorities of targeted people in the field. Additionally, they should demonstrate commitment to adhering to applicable codes of conduct, quality standards, and accountability standards by incorporating these obligations into their ongoing performance evaluations. Moreover, managers of INGOs and IDAPs should ensure that formal or informal training opportunities are available for project teams on quality and accountability standards. These training programs should also be extended to the staff of local partners. The literature widely recognizes Staff Focus as a critical aspect within INGOs and IDAPs, which presents, in turn, industry-specific challenges (Hassan et al., 2017).

The organizational values of IDAPs and implemented INGOs often revolve around principles such as equality, mentoring, and empowerment for the groups they serve. However, it is crucial for these values to be deeply ingrained within the IDAP itself and among its staff members in order for them to effectively convey these values to the targeted groups; this is particularly important in the challenging work environments and contexts of conflicts and crises. As such, some of the IDAPs are recognizing the provision of job opportunities as a core part of their assistance to the country of concern. Therefore, it is imperative to prioritize a strong focus on HR and consider it an integral part of IDAPs management and overall missions. This is what this chapter is all about!

F. I. Mahmoud Saleh and N. Karia, *Value-driven Management for International Development and Aid Projects*, https://doi.org/10.1007/978-981-97-3666-9_9

This chapter commences by shedding light on the unique considerations of staff management in IDAPs and emphasizing its paramount importance in this industry. It then delves into an examination of work-related attitudes, drawing on the latest evidence from the IDAPs literature. Additionally, the chapter explores the management of staff anxiety, morale, and stress, offering valuable insights for IDAPs managers who recruit staff from challenging operational areas and crisis contexts. Furthermore, practical determinants and steps for effectively managing diversity are provided, recognizing it as a core value and organizational competency that should be prioritized by IDAP management. Lastly, the chapter concludes by introducing practical manifestations of accountable resource utilization by IDAPs.

9.2 Special Concerns of Human Resource Management in IDAPs

As we mentioned in Chapter 2, it is not debatable for IDAPs to institutionalize and adhere to the relevant industrial best practices in humanitarian and development work. Therefore, IDAPs' staff should work according to the agreed-upon standards, objectives, performance, organizational mandate, and values, and they should be aware of the applicable policies. Furthermore, staff should adopt their competencies to accomplish their roles and expect organizations to support them in doing that.

On the other hand, the implementation of INGOs and IDAPs management should ensure that the required capacities and competencies are available within the IDAP or implementing INGO to deliver quality and added-value programs. More specifically, they should take on the following mandatory responsibilities: (1) Ensure the existence of staff policies and procedures that are transparent, fair, non-discriminatory, and aligned with local labor laws; (2) Develop clear job descriptions, objectives, and feedback procedures; (3) Enforce code of conduct to protect the affected people from discrimination and abuse; (4) Adopt organizational policies for the development of staff competencies and skills; (5) Administer policies and procedures to ensure staff well-being and security (CHS 2014).

INGOs primarily operate through project-based initiatives, which serve as the main means for accomplishing their missions (Saleh and Karia 2020). However, it is widely acknowledged that NGOs often struggle to perform effectively and experience high rates of employee turnover. As a result, these projects often fail to achieve the sustainable goals they aim for and, in turn, to add value to the lives of targeted people and communities. The successful implementation of IDAPs heavily relies on the satisfaction and commitment of staff. Therefore, various staff-related issues, including cultural and linguistic differences, recruitment and compliance with legal frameworks, compensation and performance management systems, staff well-being, travel, and turnover rates, have been identified as significant challenges within this industry. As such, staff attitudes toward their work play a vital role in TQM excellence models such as the European Foundation for Quality Management (EFQM) and critical TQM practices for NGOs. This is particularly crucial in the third sector, where high turnover rates are the norm (Walk et al. 2019).

Later in this section, we will explore the existing literature on work-related attitudes within the INGOs industry as acknowledged by the relevant literature. However, our emphasis will be first on significant practical concerns and considerations appreciated by leaders of major INGOs globally: staff satisfaction and engagement. This concern holds immense importance, as it directly impacts the overall performance and effectiveness of IDAPs. By understanding and addressing the factors that contribute to staff satisfaction and engagement, IDAPs' managers aim to create a positive work environment that fosters the productivity and success of these projects.

The professionals in the INGOs industry understand that the factors influencing staff engagement are not universal and can vary from one organization to another. Therefore, it is crucial to consider the input of staff members within IDAP to gain a comprehensive understanding of their experiences and perspectives. Additionally, it is important to consider the specific operational context when determining which factors to prioritize. By incorporating the staff voice and considering the operational context, INGOs can make informed decisions about the dimensions of staff engagement that are most relevant to their IDAP and contexts of operations and then work to address these dimensions.

For the purpose of this book, we focus on the most important drivers of staff engagement as they emerged from our field consultations, observations, and experiences. These dimensions are: (1) job engagement drivers; (2) organizational engagement drivers; and (3) individual engagement drivers. Table 9.1 outlines these three dimensions along with their relevant determinants and a summary of their practical manifestations.

Scholars have identified various attributes when conceptualizing work-related attitudes, as summarized by Karia and Saleh (2021) in Table 9.2. The most frequently mentioned attributes are job satisfaction, organizational commitment, human resource performance, job involvement, and career satisfaction. These four essential work-related attitudes in the context of INGOs and IDAPs encompass job involvement, job satisfaction, career satisfaction, and organizational commitment.

Job involvement consists of the personal involvement of the staff, interest alignment around the job, commitment to quality improvement, participation in decision-making, and regulation of detected flaws. Job satisfaction, however, consists of the way the supervisor handles staff, the competence of the supervisor in making decisions, the provision of steady employment, telling people what to do, the use of staff abilities, the operationalization of organization policies, payment and amount of work, opportunities for advancement, working conditions, and a feeling of accomplishment.

Career satisfaction encompasses several aspects, including satisfaction with career achievements, progress toward overarching career goals, opportunities for skill development and engagement in activities, utilization of skills and abilities, and the accomplishment of high-quality work.

Organizational commitment encompasses several elements, including a strong willingness to exert maximum effort for the success of the organization, advocating

Table 9.1 Dimensions of staff engagement and satisfaction

Employee engagement driver	Determinants	Practical manifestations
Job Engagement	Employee Empowerment	Employee engagement refers to the level of accountability and control employees have over their work in a supportive environment. Practical manifestations of employee engagement include conducting surveys to gather feedback, having frequent conversations with employees, setting regular check-ins, involving teams in decision-making, and providing opportunities for employees to lead passion IDAPs
	Manager Relationships	Management relationship refers to the connection between an employee and their manager, based on trust and support. Practical manifestations include regular one-on-one meetings, performance discussions, career development talks, providing context for messages from leaders, check-ins with the team, promoting autonomy, and building personal connections
	Department Leadership	Department leadership refers to the trustworthiness, transparency, and value placed on employee feedback by leaders. Practical manifestations include regular communication, utilizing various methods, providing rationale for decisions, increasing leadership visibility, customizing communications, and holding roundtables for employee input
	Career Advancement	Career advancement involves enhancing employee skills and meeting their career objectives while fulfilling organizational needs. Practical manifestations include providing resources, scheduling development days, showcasing career opportunities, reminding employees of learning resources, setting training hours, offering tools for career guidance, allocating a training budget, coaching managers, implementing internal training programs, and documenting career development plans
	Coworker Relationship	Coworker relationships involve the support and harmony among colleagues who work together. Practical manifestations include establishing backups or a buddy system, organizing team-building activities, scheduling coffee chats, promoting understanding of roles, creating a team charter, implementing peer recognition, ensuring workload visibility, providing conflict management training, and facilitating conflict resolution sessions

(continued)

Table 9.1 (continued)

Employee engagement driver	Determinants	Practical manifestations
	Recognition	Recognition involves rewarding and acknowledging employees for their outstanding performance. Practical manifestations include gathering employee feedback, increasing transparency, recognizing personal and professional achievements, evaluating and adjusting recognition programs, implementing quarterly programs, establishing clear criteria, creating peer-to-peer recognition, allocating department-level budgets, and training managers on informal recognition
Organizational Engagement	Organizational Culture	Organizational culture refers to the extent of employee alignment with the values, beliefs, and attitudes of the organization. Practical manifestations include clear communication of values, linking decisions to values, recognizing employees who embody values, defining the employee value proposition, adapting methods for remote employees, reviewing alignment with business strategy, aligning incentives, documenting cultural behaviors in virtual environments, and conducting culture assessments if needed
	INGO/IDAP Potential	INGO or IDAP potential refers to an employee's understanding, commitment, and excitement toward the organization's mission. Practical manifestations include regular organization meetings, celebrating milestones, sharing performance indicators, consistent communication, transparency, manager meetings, celebrating wins, recognizing innovation, and evaluating hiring practices
	Beneficiary Focus	Beneficiary focus involves an employee's belief in the INGOs or IDAP's ability to meet the needs of the people it serves. Practical manifestations include listening to front-line staff, gathering innovative ideas, sharing community feedback, involving leaders in front-line work, implementing a recognition program based on feedback, and prioritizing impactful interventions
	Department Collaboration	Department collaboration refers to departments working together toward a common goal. Practical manifestations include cross-collaboration, regular meetings between leaders, manager meetings, socializing opportunities, resolving conflicts, unified communication platforms, leveraging employee networks, and addressing specific departmental issues through survey data

(continued)

Table 9.1 (continued)

Employee engagement driver	Determinants	Practical manifestations
	Executive Management	Executive management involves building trust, transparency, and valuing employee feedback. Practical manifestations include ongoing communication, increased visibility, personal connections, bottom-up communication channels, consistent messaging, and acting on engagement survey feedback
	Inclusion	Inclusion aims to create a welcoming environment where employees feel valued, empowered, and able to contribute freely. Practical manifestations include establishing employee resource groups, acknowledging cultural celebrations, offering flexible time-off options, developing a diversity strategy, promoting equal opportunities for sharing ideas, reviewing policies for bias, encouraging cross-functional teams, and enhancing physical accessibility
Individual Engagement	Compensations	Compensation refers to the fairness and competitiveness of pay and benefits. Practical manifestations include providing information sessions, total reward statements, tailored benefits, conducting salary assessments, training managers, gathering market data, and seeking employee feedback
	Work–life balance	Promoting work–life balance involves updating flexible work policies, providing guidance on workload management, encouraging breaks and time off, evaluating workload distribution, gathering feedback from employees, promoting wellness resources, addressing cultural barriers, and assessing the impact of changes

for others to join and work for the organization, demonstrating loyalty to the organization, accepting any assignment to continue working for the organization, alignment between the visions of the organization and its staff, taking pride in being a part of the organization, finding inspiration in job performance, choosing to work for the organization over other options when initially joining, paying attention to the organization's future, and viewing the organization as the best choice available.

In conclusion, this book advocates that staff engagement dimensions, such as job engagement, organizational engagement, and individual engagement, play a crucial role in shaping work-related attitudes (job involvement, job satisfaction, career satisfaction, and organizational commitment) within INGOs. These work-related attitudes, in turn, directly contribute to the success, sustainability, and value-added impact of IDAPs. Accordingly, as we commenced, IDAPs and implementing INGOs leaders should make sure to consult their teams and solicit their input regularly

Table 9.2 Summary of work-related attitudes—Source: (Saleh and Karia 2020)

Work-related attitude	Author(s)
Job Satisfaction	Ooi et al. (2008), Gill et al. (2010), Hamed (2010), Prajogo and Cooper (2010), Mehra and Ranganathan (2011), Mansour and Nusairat (2012), Asaari et al. (2013), Batista et al. (2013), Liu and Liu (2014), Mosadeghrad (2014), Hanaysha (2016), Mendes and Jesus (2018), Khan et al. (2019), Addis et al. (2019), and Ahmed and Idris (2020)
Organizational Commitment	Boon et al. (2008), Mansour and Nusairat (2012), Batista et al. (2013), Asaari et al. (2013), Carlos et al. (2014), Liu and Liu (2014), Nadim and Amir (2015), Mendes and Jesus (2018), Salem et al. (2019), and Khan et al. (2019)
Human resource performance	Sivalogathasan et al. (2012), Wickramaratne (2013), Prates and Caraschi (2014), Krommuang and Suwunnamek (2015), and Heyns and Boikanyo (2019)
Job involvement	Daniel and Micaela (2007), Hamed (2010), Mansour and Nusairat (2012), and Batista et al. (2013)
Career Satisfaction	Asaari et al. (2013), Batista et al. (2013), Aktar and Pangil (2018)
Individual Performance	Carlos et al. (2014), and Khan et al. (2019)
Teamwork	Ramesh and Ravi (2013) and Khawka (2016)
Employee Satisfaction	Manhas et al. (2015) and Amin et al. (2017)
Work Conditions	Aktar and Pangil (2018)
Role clarity	Hamed (2010)
Organizational trust	Hamed (2010)
Employee relations	Kumar et al. (2009)
Work–Life Quality	Ooi et al. (2013)
Perceived job proficiency	Truitt (2011)

through the different channels and modalities in order to come up with contextual and relevant engagement action points to engage them better.

In the next section, we complement our encouragement to the leaders in this industry with further IDAPs' specific concerns that can hinder their engagement efforts.

9.3 Managing Staff Anxiety, Morale, and Stress

Working in challenging environments and crisis contexts presents an additional layer of complexity for IDAP managers. It necessitates their heightened awareness and responsiveness to the needs of their staff, who often belong to the communities being served. This responsibility extends beyond enhancing staff performance; it encompasses ensuring their safety and sustaining interventions in the face of sudden disruptions such as the COVID-19 pandemic. Drawing from my extensive experience in this field, I have personally witnessed instances where we have tragically lost team members or their loved ones. The complexities encountered in such contexts can manifest in various forms, including political (Wildeman 2017), ethical (Jackman 2018), legislative, and logistical challenges (Tirmizi and Vogelsang 2016). They may also be intertwined with ethnic conflicts (Bayiley and Teklu 2016), incidents of terrorism (Lambert 2018), language barriers (Brehm, 2019), concerns regarding the legitimacy of provided services (Noh 2018), insufficient local capacities (McEvoy et al. 2016), or perceptions regarding the intentions and relevance of assistance (Ubalijoro 2018).

Saleh and Karia (2020) have identified staff management as a crucial benchmark for effective INGO responses during the COVID-19 pandemic. In their exploration of this topic, they conducted interviews with six leaders from prominent INGOs. Interviewed leaders of INGOs have placed significant emphasis on effective staff management, particularly in relation to addressing stress, anxiety, safety, and security concerns. The feedback from interviewees highlights the recognition that IDAP teams are a crucial asset for INGOs, and therefore, their well-being and support should be prioritized during times of crisis.

The interviewees unanimously acknowledged the vital role played by staff members, with one interviewee even stating that they are the "cornerstone of our interventions." In line with this recognition, the leaders who were interviewed emphasized the crucial responsibilities of the HR department and project managers in providing culture-sensitive resources and information to support staff morale. To ensure the well-being of staff, INGOs have adopted various strategies. These include addressing common reactions that arise during outbreaks, such as fear, uncertainty, and feelings of isolation. Coping strategies for managing isolation and anxiety have been shared, along with guidance on self-care and remote work practices. By promoting healthy and safe practices, INGOs aim to create a supportive work environment that prioritizes the physical and mental well-being of their staff.

One specific example mentioned by an interviewee is the regular communication from the HR department. In response to the COVID-19 pandemic, some organizations have implemented daily email check-ins to monitor the well-being of all staff members. This proactive approach helps to maintain a sense of connection and support, even when physical interactions are limited.

In addition to addressing the immediate needs of staff, interviewees also highlighted the importance of long-term planning. They suggested revising work-from-home policies to prepare for potential future waves of COVID-19 or other crises.

This forward-thinking approach aims to ensure business continuity and resilience in the face of unforeseen challenges. However, it was noted that some staff members, particularly local partners, may lack experience in effectively utilizing virtual collaboration tools. To address this, interviewees emphasized the need for INGOs to prioritize providing training and support to enhance staff capabilities when using virtual working tools. By doing so, INGOs can ensure their business continuity and resilience in situations that require remote work.

Furthermore, interviewees stressed the importance of utilizing staff members' time during curfews or other movement restrictions. They emphasized the value of providing online courses and capacity-building opportunities to help staff enhance their skills and knowledge. This investment in staff development not only benefits individual employees but also strengthens the overall capacity of INGOs to deliver effective interventions.

Lastly, one interviewee drew attention to the specific needs of expatriate staff members who may have been separated from their families due to travel restrictions. Recognizing the emotional toll this can take, interviewees emphasized the importance of providing support and care for these individuals, ensuring they have access to resources that address their unique challenges and concerns.

Failure to address staff anxiety, morale, and stress can have detrimental effects on the success of IDAPs and the overall operations of INGOs (Smith 2018). Recognizing the significance of staff management, previous research (Saleh et al. 2017) has emphasized its role in INGO performance, particularly in terms of staff motivation, morale, security, and continuous development. The interview findings further highlight the increased importance of these aspects during times of crisis.

In light of these considerations, IDAPs' managers should consider the following operational measures during challenging or crisis contexts:

1. Vigilantly monitor and address staff stress, anxiety, and morale, extending support to both volunteers and local partners' staff (Sweis et al. 2016).
2. Increase interactions with project teams, ensuring effective communication and support during remote work situations.
3. Provide flexibility in working hours for those who require it.
4. Ensure staff members possess the necessary capabilities and training to effectively utilize the virtual and electronic tools required for remote work.

Therefore, IDAPs' leaders and their implementing INGOs must be aware of these staff-focus measures. Neglecting them can undermine the quality and accountability of IDAPs interventions and the overall success of IDAPs (Sweis et al. 2016).

9.4 Expected Behaviors of IDAP's Workers

Chapter 11 will delve into the risks associated with IDAPs and the corresponding strategies to mitigate these risks. Such as the risk of sexual harassment, exploitation, and abuse. However, this chapter focuses on specific risk mitigation concerns and strategies pertaining to social workers and resources. In this section, we first address how to articulate and tackle the expected behaviors of staff toward the targeted individuals. Subsequently, we discuss the expected behaviors within the IDAP. Lastly, we provide insights regarding the responsible utilization of resources by social workers.

9.4.1 Expected Behaviors of IDAP's Workers Toward Targeted People

Interacting with vulnerable individuals and working in crises and less developed contexts is a crucial aspect of managing IDAPs' staff. In these situations, IDAP's workers may hold a position of power over the individuals they are assisting. As a result, IDAP's managers should take these concerns into account and incorporate necessary procedures in IDAP's PM to address them and mitigate emerging risks in this regard.

The first step toward ensuring that all stakeholders of IDAPs are well-informed about the expected behaviors is to have an agreed-upon and well-communicated accountability framework. According to Saleh and Karia (2020) and Saleh and Karia (2022), the IDAPs manager should ensure that the vision, mission, and strategic goals of INGO or IDAP are well-communicated to the project's team and other stakeholders of the project. They should also be able to reinforce a serious culture toward continuous improvement, "beneficiary care," and reinforced complaints. Moreover, while the accountability framework can be defined as "the document where the commitments of INGO towards its stakeholders are stated," this document (or similar document) should be part of the IDAP's Charter or part of the implementing INGO organizational process assets or policies. Therefore, it is to be communicated with all stakeholders and considered an integral part of all IDAP's PM processes to state the expected behavior from the social workers, organizational commitments to all stakeholders, transparency, diversity and inclusion, feedback and response, participation, and continuous improvements.

The accountability framework should be endorsed by all IDAP's staff and effectively communicated to the targeted individuals. It is typically published on various communication channels to ensure that they are aware of their rights, eligibility, selection criteria, and, most importantly, how IDAP's staff should interact with them. This includes clarifying what is acceptable and what should be reported as a complaint, as well as their rights to access safe and appropriate channels for seeking assistance.

Although the objective of the accountability framework is generally similar across various IDAPs and contexts, it should be tailored to the specific operational areas, utilizing locally appropriate languages that are sensitive to gender and age.

9.4.2 Expected Behaviors Among IDAP's Workers

In the earlier section of this chapter, we examined the management of IDAPs' staff, with the aim of supporting the overall goals of IDAPs and their interactions with the communities they serve. However, in this section, we will explore an important internal aspect of IDAPs staff management, specifically the relationship between IDAPs managers and their staff concerning the expected behaviors.

This book does not claim to introduce a new paradigm for managing IDAPs. Instead, it addresses an observed dilemma within IDAPs and INGOs. This dilemma is inherited from the nature of this specific kind of project to offer strategies and practices that can enhance the lives of targeted people. This dilemma is particularly important in IDAPs that prioritize employing local staff as part of their assistance to less developed countries, as mentioned in the chapter introduction.

Based on my experience and numerous engagements with IDAPs workers as a practitioner in this field and an investigator for various team member complaints, I frequently hear staff members discussing the importance of implementing the same values that INGOs promote among their program participants to their staff as well. They often express the sentiment, "*We aspire to create a world of social justice for our beneficiaries. Why not apply this principle to us first and foremost?*" as one staff member shared. In fact, this claim can convey two important points. Firstly, it reflects the perspective of local staff who see themselves as beneficiaries of international aid. Secondly, it highlights the awareness of their rights. These two manifestations are totally right. However, it is observed that some managers, especially those from local backgrounds, may overlook or lack full awareness of these points due to their previous experiences and the management practices they have inherited from their local experience, which may have been characterized by abuse, corruption, or unfairness.

While previous experience, especially local management experience, is valuable, it is crucial for IDAPs managers at all levels to let go of traditional management practices and fully embrace international management standards. This includes being fully aware of these standards and applying them effectively. INGOs themselves should prioritize staff management by incorporating it into their onboarding packages and providing ongoing capacity building for their recruited managers. This will ensure the integration of their values and overarching goals within the organizational culture of IDAPs and fully deliver their overarching goals to the targeted communities. In contexts of chronic vulnerabilities and crises, where INGOs and international development programming are spread, these strategies will bring an indirect, multiplying, and systematic change in the overall culture across the areas and countries of operations.

Most of the standards for quality and accountability of humanitarian responses are stressed on staff-focus practices such as empowerment and wellness (Saleh and Karia 2020). However, these standards can be manipulated, especially in contexts where corruption is prevalent. We have observed numerous instances where employees themselves may abuse these principles by filing complaints against their colleagues or supervisors. As a result, senior management teams, HR staff, and investigators must possess sufficient expertise and local knowledge to distinguish between genuine and false allegations whenever they arise, especially in cases involving protection from sexual exploitation, harassment, and abuse. In order to safeguard everyone involved, it is crucial to establish a comprehensive set of measures and penalties, ensuring that all individuals are aware of them. For instance, INGOs might offer policies for flexible work arrangements. Such policies should be closely monitored and associated with specific guidelines or conditions that avoid any potential misuse or manipulation toward the ultimate accountability of operations.

9.5 Managing Diversity

Diversity is not limited to age, gender, skin color, or religion. Humans, however, are different in many aspects that build what is called "identity." In fact, identity is formulated from multidimensional factors. Each person has a different human experience, a different current or previous social or economic class, a different educational background, a different job position, a different religious orientation, a different nationality, a different gender, a different age group, a different working experience, a different personality, a different way of thinking, a different surrounding society, different relationships and connections, different qualities, and even different deficiencies; all these factors and others, therefore, formulate the identity of each human. As a result, each individual will have a distinguished identity from others in the system in which she or he is present, whether it be a workplace or any other system.

This book focuses on exploring the managerial aspects of diversity rather than delving into ideological or political matters. Given that religions and developed countries have their own teachings and laws regarding diversity and identity differences, we explicitly state that the discussions and examples presented in this section are solely intended for the purposes of this book and its managerial scope.

In any given system, an individual's identity can either enhance or diminish their position. For instance, being an Indian or Middle Eastern male from a specific tribal background within a particular age group or high economic class can grant greater power in a specific context, as opposed to a female being from another tribal background, economic class, or age group. However, this power dynamic can drastically change if the same identities transition to another system or context. This implies that power dynamics, whether elevated or diminished, are subject to significant shifts when individuals move to different systems.

We believe, as the authors of this book, that simply thinking that you have more power than others because of your different identity is something that should not exist in the first place. Once a person believes in these differences, it is considered a deficiency in the concepts of human justice and diversity in this person. However, the managers of IDAPs and leaders of INGOs should be aware of these concepts in order to ensure their organizations manage diversity to the fullest. Being a member of a power-up in an organization means that you and your group determine the norms in this organization, and your actions are considered acceptable and customary, while those who are in power-down positions should be obliged to follow the norms and customary rules set by the group of power-ups.

The advanced entities that compete and strive to excel on the international stage, whether they are countries or organizations, make efforts to bridge the gap between those in positions of power and those who are not. For instance, the White House offices recruit employees from diverse backgrounds, encompassing different origins, ethnicities, and orientations. This approach is also reflected in American embassies. I vividly recall my American visa interview over a decade ago in one of the Gulf countries. The staff consisted of a lady of Palestinian descent who inspected the entrants, a man of Lebanese origin who verified their identities, an elderly man with dark skin, and three other employees of East Asian, Indian, and European backgrounds. Similar diversity can be observed in the restaurants found in global cities like Istanbul, where you encounter employees of Arab, Indian, and Turkish origins. The diversity of staff in these two examples is not only about the physical distribution. But to better serve the business goals of both entities, White House, therefore, strives to serve its foreign policies through this diversity by integrating different perspectives. The Istanbul restaurant strives to accommodate its different customers by speaking their languages when required and adapting to their different moods in food.

The fundamental approach to managing diversity in IDAPs should be grounded in the targeted people and communities. IDAPs target diverse communities and people. Therefore, they must be diverse by themselves in order to match the diverse needs of their targeted groups and, in turn, to meet their expectations to the maximum extent. To that end, the rest of this section provides some essential strategies that should be under the radar of IDAPs managers in order to better manage workplace diversity in these projects and, in turn, to add value to the lives of targeted people.

First of all, IDAPs should make sure to hire staff from different backgrounds to match the diversity of targeted people in terms. For instance, the IDAPs managers should act intentionally to have managers, not only staff, from different social and economic classes. In most cases, those managers are better able to understand, analyze, and respond to the targeted people from these marginalized groups. This strategy should not only be on the practice level, but also on the organizational systems level, such as HR policies, recruitment procedures, and staff appraisal systems within the IDAPs to ensure the operationalization and manifestation of diversity practices.

Leaders and managers at all levels should act as role models in order to mainstream diversity at all organizational levels. As a manager working in an IDAP, you should make sure to spend equal time talking to my staff and colleagues from different backgrounds, gender groups, age groups, education levels, and organizational levels to ensure the capturing of diverse contributions. Likewise, you should ensure the existence of safe spaces to express all opinions; this includes meetings, discussions, workshops, and any form of interaction in the IDAP.

Despite having good diversity within the INGOs or IDAPs, the leaders should be aware of any bad attitudes or behaviors against diversity, even facial expressions, body language, and voice tones. Such expressions should be firmly stopped and even investigated as needed.

Diversity and inclusion should also be integrated into all business practices. This includes, but is not limited to, outreach activities, communication channels, partnerships, and procurement procedures. It is not irrelevant at all for IDAPs managers to ensure diversity within their portfolio of suppliers, sub-grantees, and local partners. As the author of this book, I worked for one of the IDAPs that targeted a town in a Middle Eastern country that consisted of two major community parts. Therefore, while we were in need of having one partnership with one of the local community-based organizations, we made sure to establish partnerships with two organizations, each of them dominated by a board from a different community group, in order to be sensitive to any potential conflict in the area of operations.

9.6 Accountable Use of Resources

Just as there are unique considerations when managing human resources in IDAPs, the management of non-human resources also requires attention. This is essential to ensure the responsible utilization of IDAP's resources and to contribute effectively to the organization's mission of supporting vulnerable and underdeveloped communities.

To that end, this chapter concludes with the provision of practical recommendations to ensure the efficient use of resources and the avoidance of corruption and misuse of IDAP's resources. These practices, however, are essential for IDAP's managers to integrate into the resource management processes of the PM model adopted by IDAPs to deliver its goals and objectives as follows:

1. Write down the workflows (if you do not have SOPs) and evaluate each step, including approvals needed, people involved, and required inputs for each step. Ask the question: Is all of this really necessary? Where can we insert a shortcut? For instance, what can be done online instead of paperwork?
2. Define the major categories of expenditure as part of the plan resources process; utilities and office supplies are usually payments that become routine. If it is worth reviewing them; Are we getting the best offers? Are we actually consuming the mobile and/or internet bundles we bought? And so on.
3. Plan and review regularly. Take the time to make plans involving all departments; all input is useful; listen to what others have to say. Stick to the plan and review it regularly during the execution of the project to make sure everything is on track. It is good to assign one focal point that facilitates this process.
4. Use technology: there are many free online tools that can be used to increase efficiency. I recall that we reduced the cost of fuel by 42% by utilizing a fleet management system. Using online tools where different users can insert their information spares you the time of planning for hotel bookings, airport pickups, and other expenses.

5. Train your team on proper documentation; don't only rely on finance to give instructions. Explain to your team that proper documentation protects them before it protects the organization's resources. Therefore, training on documentation is to be added to all processes of resource management.
6. As the project manager, be a role model when using and documenting IDAP's resources.
7. Trust others and delegate tasks, but make others accountable.
8. Set clear policies that identify the gray areas and explain what can be considered fraud.
9. Apply good governance, segregation of duties, plan resource management processes (see the Generally Accepted Accounting Principles GAAP), and ensure proper financial systems.
10. Use of technology: invest in systems—information management systems and configuration management systems.
11. Choose your team carefully, and also provide fair salaries and incentives.
12. Invest in the work environment, make it a comfortable one, open channels, and the well-being of staff are very important. If employees like their jobs, corruption is less likely.
13. Make sure to ask about the history of staff and partners concerning fraud and breaching the code of conduct when doing reference checks.

References

Bayiley YT, Teklu GK (2016) Success factors and criteria in the management of international development projects. Int J Manag Proj Bus 9(3):562–582

Brehm MV (2019) Respecting communities: languages and cultural understanding in international development work. Dev Pract 29(4):534–537

Core Humanitarian Standard (CHS) (2014) Core humanitarian standard on quality and accountability. HAP International, People in Aid, and the Sphere Project, Geneva

Hassan MM, Bashir S, Abbas SM (2017) The impact of project managers' personality on project success in NGOs: the mediating role of transformational leadership. Proj Manag J 48(2):74–87

Jackman M (2018) Reaching out: navigating the ethical, legislative, and physical obstacles to providing assistance to migrants in Morocco. Independent Study Project (ISP) Collection, SIT Study Abroad, p 2835

Karia N, Saleh FIM (2021) The effect of TQM practices on INGOs' staff work-related attitudes. Benchmarking Int J 29(2):596–621

Lambert KM (2018) Assessing the impact of the political environment on INGO vulnerability to terrorist attack. Risk, Hazards and Crisis in Public Policy 9(4):431–454

McEvoy P, Brady M, Munck R (2016). Capacity development through international projects: a complex adaptive systems perspective. Int J Manag Proj Bus 9(3):528–545

Noh JE (2018) The legitimacy of development nongovernmental organisations as global citizenship education providers in Korea. Educ Citizsh Soc Justice 14(3):241–259

Saleh FIM, Karia N (2020) Management for international development and aid projects: A new conceptual model. Nonprofit Manag Leadersh 31(2):373–386

Saleh FI, Karia N (2022) Adaptive project management model for the international development and aid projects. Nonprofit Manag Leadersh 33(2):383–409

Saleh FIM, Sweis RJ, Abdelqader BY, Abdallah AB, Arafeh M (2017) The effect of TQM dimensions on the performance of international non-governmental organizations operating in Jordan. Int J Prod Qual Manag 21(4):443–459

Smith AN (2018) Foreign aid and development in the democratic republic of the Congo: an analysis of international barriers to development. Perceptions 4(2):19

Sweis RJ, Saleh FIM, Dahiyat SE, Sweis NJ, Saleh RA, Diab H (2016) Benchmarking of TQM practices in INGOs: a literature review. Benchmarking Int J 23(1):236–261

Tirmizi SA, Vogelsang JD (eds) (2016) Leading and managing in the social sector: strategies for advancing human dignity and social justice. Springer

Ubalijoro É (2018) Transforming community through feminine leadership. In Leadership and power in international development: navigating the intersections of gender, culture, context, and sustainability. Emerald Publishing Limited, 83–97

Walk M, Zhang R, Littlepage L (2019) "Don't you want to stay?" The impact of training and recognition as human resource practices on volunteer turnover. Nonprofit Manag Leadersh 29(4):509–527

Wildeman J (2017) Undermining the democratic process: the Canadian government suppression of Palestinian development aid projects. Can J Middle East Stud 2(1):2033

Chapter 10
Management of Donors

10.1 Introduction

As the author of this book, I am writing this chapter on the next day of the bombing of the Baptist Church's Baptist Hospital in Gaza, which resulted in the loss of nearly 500 lives, with the majority being women and children. This bombing happened after two weeks of continuous conflict in Gaza between the Israeli armed forces and the Palestinian resistance.

I work as the director of one of the largest USAID programs in Jordan, a country that has the highest number of Palestinian refugees and displaced individuals who fled to Jordan in 1948 and 1976. Many people in Jordan accuse the United States, the donor of our program, of being a partner to Israel in its military operations against Gaza. This morning, our country director, who is American, visited my office to check in and discuss the possibility of allowing our staff to work from home due to nearby protests in order to ensure their safety. I explained to him that the issue not only involves movement restrictions in the neighborhood but also the emotional impact on our staff and their families due to the ongoing events in the region. At the end of the day, we decided to provide the option for team members who may feel particularly vulnerable or sensitive to working from home and being with their families during these challenging times.

Two days later, we observed a moment of silence to honor the souls of the victims of this conflict. During this moment, numerous colleagues requested permission to express their beliefs, knowing that they were part of a program funded by the United States. In the previous chapter, we discussed the perception of IDAPs' staff and the employment of national staff as part of the international aid provided by these projects. This, therefore, brings the management of donors and their mandates through the national lenses as an essential part of value-added management for IDAPs; the thing which we discuss in this chapter, and has been widely acknowledged by the literature as a major dimension of complexity for managing IDAPs

F. I. Mahmoud Saleh and N. Karia, *Value-driven Management for International Development and Aid Projects*, https://doi.org/10.1007/978-981-97-3666-9_10

(Wildeman 2017; Haapala and Keskinen 2018; Martinez and Cooper 2017; Kloster 2019).

This chapter commences with answering the question of why to manage donors, then moves on to provide different modalities and actions to operationalize this important part of IDAPs management. As the management of donors can differ based on the setting and context of operations, we then provide specific practical practices on how to manage donors, first in the contexts of emergency responses, then in the nexus programming settings, and in the pure development programming to ensure retaining donors and keep momentum for the needs of targeted people, communities, and countries. Lastly, this chapter concludes by providing specific project management processes that can be adopted and integrated into the project management policies and procedures of the implementing INGO.

10.2 Why Manage Donors

Donors are the primary source of funding for INGOs, serving as intermediaries between the donors and the targeted communities. In previous chapters, we unpacked the issue of accountability for INGOs toward the communities they serve, which arises due to this intermediary role. In this chapter, however, we delve deeper into the value-added management of IDAPs throughout their management cycle.

The value-added management of IDAPs is all about going beyond the limited view of the success of the projects regarding closing the projects within the planned scope, time, and cost. Therefore, consider the broader social and organizational aspects of the project (Saleh and Karia 2022) for the ultimate interest of targeted people and communities. Likewise, consider the different stakeholders in a balanced manner, particularly when it comes to balancing the attention between program participants from one side and the donors from the other side.

Both modern management approaches and industrial standards such as TQM and the Quality Criteria of CHS gave greater attention to service recipients and crisis-affected people than to donors. Despite the goodness of this humanitarian sense, donors are still key stakeholders and part of the accountability equation that needs to be addressed by IDAPs managers. However, IDAPs usually fall into the trap of giving the highest attention to their donors to secure funds and often adopt the views and priorities of their donors' regarding the needs of communities, which might lead to non-needs-based interventions (Aldashev and Navarra 2018) as well as diminishing the decision-making ability of the targeted groups (Penn 2019).

INGOs implement their strategic missions through donor-funded projects (Anderson and Lannon 2018). However, the competition among INGOs has increased in order to get the already shrinking funds of donors. At the same time, the evaluation of grants has started to be performance-based instead of project-based, which entails further complexities that, if not managed fairly, will cause the failure of IDAPs (Brehm 2019), particularly if these complexities are associated with the existence of gaps between donors' agendas and the realities on the ground (Kloster 2019).

Within this sector, quality is generally defined by the satisfaction of both donors and beneficiaries. Furthermore, donor retention has been acknowledged as a key dimension for IDAPs success, which in turn requires these projects to keep their donors satisfied in order to ensure the continuity of funds to finance their interventions aiming to respond to the needs of targeted people and underdeveloped countries. This, therefore, makes the management of donors a key discipline for the value-added management of IDAPs (Saleh et al. 2017).

10.3 How to Manage Donors

The interaction between technical aspects of international development and aid on one side, and political factors on the other is crucial for understanding and rationalizing the mandates and agendas of international donors. As a result, these mandates and agendas cannot be fully interpreted without considering the political aspects of governments and corporations involved in the IDAPs. However, this dilemma requires separate, in-depth discussions in order to be fully unpacked. This book, therefore, focuses solely on the technical reflections of these mandates and agendas and, in turn, the emerging formats of donors' aims in this regard.

Despite the underlying political factors of international development and aid, donors' agendas, and the forms of donor support can vary to respond to a wide spectrum of interventions, starting from pure emergency responses to human-made crises or natural disasters, and ending macro-economy support to underdeveloped and developing countries and regions. Based on that, the strategies and actions to manage donors vary as well.

As the author of this book, I worked in different settings of IDAPs, such as, but not limited to, emergency and lifesaving responses, dual nexus programming between emergency and development interventions, triple nexus programming that connects the emergency responses with the development and peacebuilding programs, and lastly, pure development programs. In the rest of this section, therefore, we provide some key practical strategies for interacting with donors and managing their expectations across this spectrum of nexuses in the different stages of IDAPs' lifecycle.

10.3.1 Manage Donors in Emergency Responses

Regardless of the emergency types that IDAPs respond to, the top priority is always saving the lives of affected people in crises. Donors, therefore, are expected not to be sophisticated in their contractual requirements with responding INGOs and to be satisfied with the minimum level of reporting.

On the day of writing this section, as a practitioner in an INGO in the Middle East, I discussed with a colleague in our M&E department the accountability requirements for a proposed distribution of cash assistance and non-food items to internally displaced people in Gaza. This distribution is intended for those who have fled their homes due to the ongoing war, resulting in hunger and a lack of basic needs for over 45 days. The distribution process is complex and risky, as it aims to reach thousands of people who have lost their homes and family members. We concluded that rough estimations of the targeted numbers and counting the number of distributions, but not the benefited people, should be sufficient to be communicated and committed to this potential donor.

In crisis situations, donors might urgently need to be informed about the situation of the crisis and affected people to secure and transfer funds as quickly as possible to save lives and stop the bleeding of losses. Accordingly, INGOs should conduct rapid needs assessments and gender analyses to capture the situation of affected people, including the number of affected men, women, boys, and girls, along with specific gender and age needs. This should also include the specific immediate needs of these groups, such as food items, non-food items, medical requirements, and hygiene materials. Conflict sensitivity analysis should also be conducted whenever it is applicable.

To that end, INGOs should exploit their presence and experience in the areas of operations to capture any already existing data or to collect the required primary data in order to share it with their potential donors as quickly as possible for exploring the available donors' funds for the purpose of designing the proposed responses to these urgent needs.

After INGOs mobilize the necessary resources and secure funds from their donors to initiate the IDAPs, it is essential to keep the donors regularly informed of the response progress beyond the contractual reporting. This should be accomplished by sharing regular situational reports that show the total number of affected people as well as the number of individuals who have been reached out of that total.

Once the situation on the ground allows, IDAPs leaders can arrange field visits to the donors' representatives to be able to witness the needs of the affected population and the direct effects of donations on the ground. This, however, will allow donors to be fully aware of the situation and ensure the flow of support for the ongoing operations and potential further emergency donations alike. However, this kind of communication and management needs to be moved to a different paradigm as the crisis of concern extends with time. Donors and all stakeholders will be interested in witnessing the early recovery signs, rehabilitation behaviors, and how targeted people started to cope positively with the shocks. This, therefore, will pave the way for IDAPs' leaders to move to the next layer of donors' management practices and, more specifically, to start managing donors using the lens of nexus programming, as we will discuss in the next sub-section.

10.3.2 Manage Donors in Nexus Programming

In this section, we unpack the strategies for managing donors in both the dual nexus and the triple nexus. By double nexus, we mean the linkage between emergency responses and development programming. Once the crisis starts to take on a protracted nature, the implementing INGOs should start to pursue early recovery and stabilization of targeted people or entities in the designs of their IDAPs. Therefore, it creates preconditions for development and builds resilience capacities to resist future shocks and crises.

Resilience, as a keyword for nexus programming, is generally defined as the ability to cope with and recover from shocks and find ways to manage future shocks using available resources or asking for support when needed. This definition, however, can be applied to people, communities, businesses, organizations, and market systems, as all are potential targeted segments for IDAPs.

Regardless of the type of targeted entities identified by the IDAP, the initial response should be focused first on ensuring continuity in the short term. Then, nurture emerging needs as a medium-term strategy before reaching the final long-term strategy of resilience concerning the creation of genuinely new capabilities of targeted entities (Markopoulos et al. 2019). In this regard, we highlight two frameworks that can be applied to both individuals and organizations in terms of nexus programming and its managerial aspects. These frameworks are CARE International's resilience framework (CARE International 2016) and McKinsey's horizon model (Markopoulos et al. 2019).

CARE's International Resilience Marker focuses on individuals or households and defines resilience as "managing risk and dealing with shocks and stresses that negatively influence people's lives." This marker requires the first identification and analysis of vulnerabilities to shocks and stresses in the context of IDAP. Then, it asks if the IDAP responds to the top three shocks and risks identified, and then, it moves to assess if the IDAP strengthens assets as well as the most significant drivers of risk that cause people to deal with shocks and risks identified. In its next question, the marker asks about the ability of IDAP to influence the rules, plans, policies, or legislation to increase the resilience of vulnerable individuals and communities to these shocks. Last, the marker assesses if the IDAP is able to consider the potentially harmful effects of its activities that could intensify or create new risks for the targeted people.

The flow of resilience, and in turn, the nexus response, therefore, covers the spectrum that starts from identifying and responding to shocks and risks and ends with addressing the underlying causes and system-level rules for these shocks and risks. Accordingly, donors should be informed about the emergent deliverables and evidence associated with these stages of nexus programming throughout the life cycle of IDAP. This should include, but is not limited to, keeping donors informed about how the IDAP adapts its internal processes, work modalities, partnerships, and coordination required to meet the requirements of resilience and nexus programming. As such, the IDAPs and implementing INGOs might also be required to develop and share with their donors their operational strategies that govern these processes and work modalities as part of their proposals and regular reporting alike.

On the other hand, McKinsey's three-horizons model focuses on organizational business continuity. This model has been widely adopted across the board (Markopoulos et al. 2019), as well as by Saleh and Karia (2020) in the context of dealing with the unexpected end of IDAPs due to COVID-19 and aiming for the expansion of these projects after the pandemic. This is to meet the short and longer-term needs of people and organizational alike. In a similar structure of the resilience structure for individuals and households, McKinsey's model addresses business continuity when facing shocks, then nurtures the emerging needs and complexities while considering the exploitation of learnings and new capacities for building the new normal of business to deal with future risks and grow.

According to Saleh and Karia (2020), IDAPs and implementing INGOs should first focus on their "Business Continuity Plans." Thus, INGOs operationalize it by keeping people safe and maintaining programming as much as they can; further, to keep donors notified about the status of their funded projects. Accordingly, these plans should be dealt with as live documents and critical communications tools for all the internal and external stakeholders. This, in turn, will maintain the ultimate transparency and accountability of INGOs' interventions with donors. In the early stages of crises, IDAPs should keep close communication with their donors and prioritize the following strategies concerning the management of their donors:

- Close monitoring of contractual obligations and the effect of sudden crises on the IDAP's operations.
- Share the updated risk management and business continuation plans with the donors.
- Discuss the potential repurposing of current interventions as well as the possible specific funding for responding to the emerging shocks and risks.
- Establish and maintain the required local partnerships and networks for crisis management, and find ways to engage them in ongoing and upcoming interventions to ensure local ownership, resilience, and sustainability.
- Detailed staff assignments, in particular those who work remotely, are necessary to maintain accountable cost allocations.

Once these strategies are realized, IDAPs should start working on longer-term strategies to deal with the emerging shocks and risks, focusing on the following strategies:

- Document all of the lessons learned that emerged from the pandemic and identify and improve the newly emerged activities and modalities of implementation.
- Maintain and institutionalize what worked well for permanent adoption.
- Reviewing program standard operation procedures (SOPs) and program support internal policies and procedures in terms of their ability to respond to the newly adopted approaches.
- Develop concepts as well as a list of potential supporters to address the emerging consequences of targeted groups due to the emerging shocks and risks.

- Developing organizational strategies and resources that can address the longer-term aspects of community resilience and preparedness for any future risks or crises.
- Proactively communicating potential changes with donors and other stakeholders while continually seeking their feedback.

The triple nexus connects emergency responses with development and peacebuilding factors toward holistic outcomes and over extended timeframes. Peacebuilding is a set of post-conflict interventions that aim to address the root causes of conflicts and rebuild all dimensions of affected societies in the aftermath of crises to repair the damage and trust among these dimensions and support processes that will continue once the emergency situation starts to stabilize.

First of all, the peacebuilding programs and triple nexus programming should be community-driven and, in turn, value-driven to address the root causes of affected populations. This should start with identifying the collective outcomes and building a common understanding and agreement with all stakeholders on these outcomes at the national level.

Once these determinants are fulfilled, the implementing INGO can start conceptualizing the lasting intended peace toward ending the current state of negative peace and moving to a future state of positive peace. This conceptualization, however, can be the core evidence and, in turn, the theory of change for the funding requests from donors to initiate and implement triple nexus IDAPs.

During the implementation of nexus IDAPs and at the end of these projects, the management should communicate with their donors how the supported IDAPs worked on the causal relationships between emergency, development, and peacebuilding. Causal relationships, however, should focus on how the development preconditions have been built due to emergency responses, how positive peacebuilding is achieved by realizing development outcomes, and how development outcomes are sustained by the positive peacebuilding created.

10.3.3 Manage Donors in Pure Development Programming

Generally speaking, INGOs authorize IDAPs to respond to social needs, such as supporting water management systems, sanitation, education, and the provision of help to communities suffering from infectious diseases (PMI 2017), as well as to meet the globally agreed-upon Sustainable Development Goals (SDGs) that are unable to be achieved yet (Anderson 2017). The SDGs are all about addressing the global challenges for all people around the globe, including, but not limited to, poverty, inequality, environmental degradation, climate change, peace and justice, and prosperity. According to the UN (2019), the seventeen agreed-upon SDGs are: (1) no poverty; (2) zero hunger; (3) good health and well-being; (4) quality education; (5) gender equality; (6) clean water and sanitation; (7) affordable and clean energy; (8) decent work and economic growth; (9) industry innovation and infrastructure;

(10) reduce inequalities; (11) sustainable cities and communities; (12) responsible production and consumption; (13) climate action; (14) life below water; (15) life on land; (16) peace, justice, and strong institutions; and (17) partnerships for the goals.

Responding to the SDGs involves a variety of practical manifestations and the nature of activities for IDAPs. Therefore, it might in form of response to emerged consequences of crises (Oliver-Smith 2019), poverty alleviation (Forkuor and Agyemang 2018; Nhapi 2019), promote human rights (Ayoyo 2019), post-disaster recovery, reconstruction, and restoration (Vahanvati and Mulligan 2017), response to rural–urban and climate-induced migrations (Ji 2018), education of global citizenship and integration of immigrants (Noh 2018), educational development (Zapp 2019), food security (Rudnick et al. 2019), agricultural education and training (Gill et al. 2017), urban development (Harms 2017), sport for development and peace (Schulenkorf 2017), water management (Haapala and Keskinen 2018), electricity and energy (Tang 2019), community self-reliance and institutional governance (McEvoy et al. 2016), early childhood (Penn 2019), child protection, and family-based care (Fronek et al., 2019), protection of cultural heritage (Munawar 2019), reproductive health development (Dumrak et al. 2017), or building the governmental and institutional systems (McEvoy et al. 2016).

Regardless of the aim of development programs, the requirements of donors are sophisticated and more complex than those of humanitarian or nexus programs. As a result, IDAPs managers are expected to meet these requirements due to the longer timeframes involved in designing, planning, and implementing development programs.

In addition to the sophistication of contractual requirements, the management of donors in development programming is characterized by flexibility toward ensuring sustainability as a shared goal of the different sectors, which in fact is inherited from the nature of this kind of programming. This means that the detailed requirements could not be definitively designed or planned from the conceptualization or initiation phases of IDAPs but need to be built up as the IDAPs go. Therefore, the conceptualization processes and definitive planning are usually part of the IDAP's lifecycle itself, regardless of the adopted PM methodology. The rest of this section unpacks the key donor management aspects across the general stages of IDAPs' lifecycle.

The Conceptualization Stages

Before the initiation of IDAPs and as part of the fundraising submission packages, the implementing INGOs should be able to provide their potential donors with enough evidence of the national development priorities in the country of operations and the underlying causes of poverty. This is necessary to justify the proposed development interventions. Additionally, the development of national development strategies and collaboration with national governments can be part of IDAP's design.

Usually, the key international development donors and agencies have their own development strategies for the developing countries of operations. These strategies are expected to address the main priorities of the country of concern. For instance, the USAID mission in Jordan, which is the largest USAID mission in the world, has a dimensional development strategy for maintaining Jordan's stability and building self-reliance; it is called the Country Development Cooperation Strategy (CDCS). Jordan's CDCS objectives are: (1) inclusive private sector-led growth; (2) Jordan's ability to improve water security; (3) equitable, democratic governance; (4) human potential; and (5) agency and leadership of women. Therefore, the conceptualization of business cases and proposals of applicants for USAID's funds must be aligned with at least one of these objectives, and build their monitoring, evaluation, and learning plans using their indicators wherever they can to get funds and facilitate approvals of interventions.

Development programs are mostly long-term programs, in which "sustainability" is the key word in such kinds of programming. This, however, makes the engagement of local actors and specialized development for-profit or non-profit actors a key factor of success when communicating IDAPs concepts with international development donors. While the prime contractors or sub-grantees should show their ability to manage the proposed consortium, they should also be able to show the specific added value of each consortium member. Furthermore, those local partners and specialized development actors with good records of success should be prioritized when selecting consortium members. Getting a sense of donors' perceptions about the different technical areas, implementation approaches, and local partners is essential to be done as early as possible before formally submitting proposals for development donors whenever it is possible.

Last, and based on our analogous experience as authors of this book, we constantly advise the applicants to international development donors to focus on "impact at scale," systems-level development solutions, and policy change as constant talking points when interacting with their potential donors to match the huge investments they have and well justify the proposed investments.

The Execution Stage

The execution phase of global development projects involves the most extensive management efforts, interactions, and communication with donors. This stage may involve identifying specific target groups, determining implementation strategies, mapping relevant stakeholders, and establishing necessary partnerships. Consequently, the majority of IDAP deliverables are provided, and most adjustments are made during this phase. Therefore, it is essential to closely manage donors to expedite approvals and accomplish these tasks.

Given the focus on development programming, which emphasizes not only outcomes but also processes, it is crucial to keep donors engaged in various aspects of the work and milestones. As the author of this book and practitioner in the non-profit industry, I used to invite donor representatives to participate in design workshops and "Pause and Reflect" sessions to ensure proactive reflection and garner their support during these crucial moments. This approach significantly streamlines the approval process and leverages the donors' ability to influence in-country governments when necessary. Additionally, I regularly invited donor representatives to all events and ceremonies, not only to show their support for these occasions but also to witness the impact of interventions and hear the stories of the people targeted by these efforts firsthand.

As previously mentioned, donors have their own coordination platforms that regularly bring together their implementing partners for coordination. For example, UN agencies have sectoral working groups aimed at establishing sectoral objectives and assessing collective sectoral impacts. Similarly, USAID's missions have coordination platforms for development pillars, such as monthly meetings for the Chief of Parties and a community of practices that bring together thematic competencies to streamline and enhance implementation methods continually. Therefore, IDAPs managers must ensure active participation in these platforms, not only to meet donor expectations but also to ensure coordinated targeting and an inclusive impact of collective interventions.

Finally, new technologies like online Customer Relationship Management (CRM) systems and progress monitoring dashboards are highly recommended as proven strategies for managing IDAP donors and keeping them informed about implementation progress and the added value of their funds. Therefore, it is not unusual for transparent IDAP leaders to provide their donors with real-time access to information about implementation progress, contractual obligations, and the impact of funds and interventions on the lives of targeted individuals.

Closeout and Post-IDAPs Stages

The project-based structures of INGOs can ensure the highest level of commitment and focus of resources on achieving the objectives of IDAPs. However, INGOs that adopt these structures can fall into the trap of losing the longer-term momentum of poverty reduction and sustainable development goals in the country of operations and their own superior strategic goals alike. Therefore, the wise INGOs and smart leaders of IDAPs should avoid such traps by using the longer-term lenses of development objectives when closing and transiting the IDAPs. Therefore, we suggest the following practical strategies to be undertaken during the closeout and post-IDAP stages, not only to inform the upcoming donors' strategies and funds but also to provide evidence-based learning to other development actors alike:

- **Share and document findings**: Whether required by contract or not, publishing IDAP reports should be a priority for INGOs during the closeout stages. This should be a standard practice for all INGOs to demonstrate transparency to stakeholders and the public. Therefore, any assessments, research, and insights from IDAP implementation should be shared on donors' or INGOs' platforms. Specific programmatic and policy recommendations should be emphasized to ensure meaningful dissemination of these findings.
- **Donor's retention plan**: IDAP's missions should not be limited to the lifecycle of the project; this is not only essential for sustaining the funds but also for ensuring commitment to the needs of targeted entities. All that we have discussed in this chapter benefits INGOs in retaining their donors, but the documentation of this intention should be prioritized as part of the closeout phase of IDAP to ensure operationalizing it through specific action plans and resources. Therefore, we suggest developing what is called a "donor's retention plan," a plan that sets specific actions for keeping donors informed about the needs of targeted entities,

development opportunities in the context of operations, and the updated strategies of INGOs to respond to these needs and opportunities.

- **Invest in ex-post evaluation**: This kind of evaluation takes place a couple of years after the project and aims to measure the ultimate long-term impacts of the IDAP. It usually is not allocated as part of the IDAP's budget but should be done by the implementing INGOs themselves. This investment will not only prove the commitment of INGOs to the international sustainable development goals, but it will also inform the INGOs themselves and other development actors when conceptualizing future IDAPs and development interventions in the interest of adding value to the needs of targeted people, communities, and countries of concern.

10.4 Project Management Processes for Managing Donors

Through this chapter, we discussed the complexity of managing IDAP's donors and the alignment of their mandates with the realities of the contexts of operations. We also highlighted some important aspects of the relevancy of donors' management to the IDAPs, and lastly, we discussed how to manage donors in the different contexts and work settings of IDAPs. This section, however, concludes that these discussions include the provision of systematic processes that can be used by IDAP's managers and INGOs leaders to integrate donor management as part of their project and program management policies and procedures as introduced by Saleh and Karia (2022).

Saleh and Karia (2022) outlined three interlinked processes for MEAL functions that aim collectively to align donors' agendas with local realities, satisfy donors, and ensure the continuity of their support. To that end, they critiqued the PMBOK® Guide and adapted its stakeholder knowledge area as follows (See Fig. 10.1).

- To amend the "stakeholder management plan" by adding a new tool to "identify stakeholders." This tool aims to identify the donor's mandate, agendas, priorities, and policies.
- To add a new process (plan donor satisfaction) to the planning process group (stakeholder management knowledge area), analyze the donor's agendas in line with the local context and realities of the project, and use traditional inputs, tools, and techniques for planning processes. However, the suggested output of this process is the "donor management plan," which should state the following:
  - Actions to align donor's agendas with the local realities.
  - Actions to follow up and track the achievements of donors' priorities.
  - Actions to communicate with the donor, keep him updated, and identify responsibilities in this regard.
  - Actions to arrange donor's field visits (if applicable) and keep him posted about the successes and challenges.

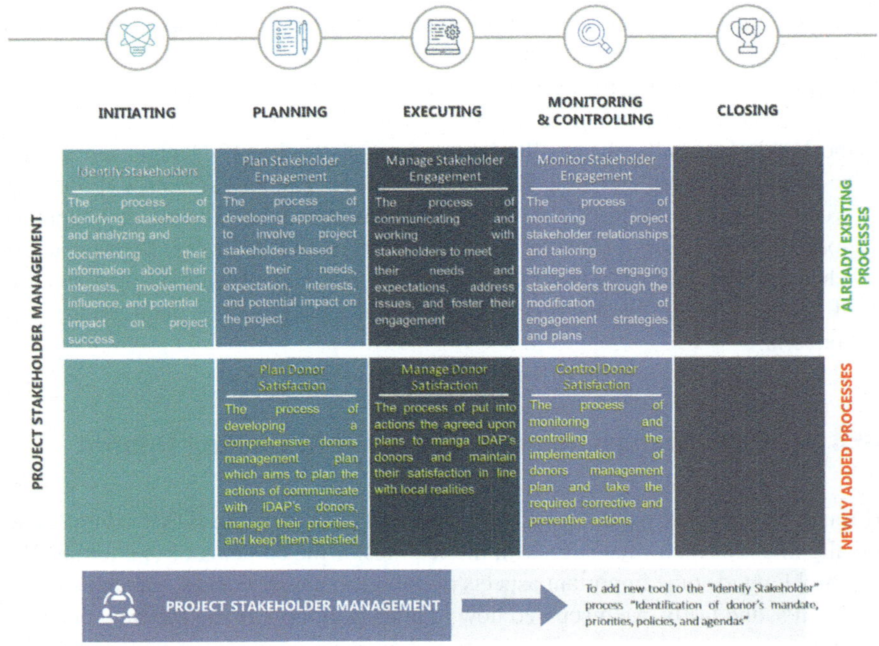

Fig. 10.1 Description and placement of proposed adaptations

  – Actions to keep donors satisfied and to lay the foundation for his continuous support and cooperation with them.

- Add traditional processes to the executing process group (stakeholder management knowledge area) to manage the donor management plan and manage donor satisfaction.
- Add the traditional monitoring and controlling process to the stakeholder management knowledge area) to control donor management plan, "control Donor Satisfaction" process.

References

Aldashev G, Navarra C (2018) Development NGOS: basic facts. Ann Public Coop Econ 89(1):125–155

Anderson RE (2017) Well-being, future generations, and prevention of suffering from climate change. Alleviating world suffering. Springer, Cham, pp 431–448

Anderson K, Lannon J (2018) Project management performance assessment in the non-profit sector. Proj Manag Res Pract 5:1–20

Ayoyo DD (2019) INGOs/IGOs and the diffusion of human rights: practices, prospects, and perils. Soc Mov Stud 18(3):381–384

Brehm V (2019) Respecting communities: languages and cultural understanding in international development work. Dev Pract 29(4):534–537
CARE International (2016) Increasing resilience: theoretical guidance document for CARE international. https://careclimatechange.org/cares-resilience-marker/
Dumrak J, Baroudi B, Hadjinicolaou N (2017) Exploring the association between project management knowledge areas and sustainable outcomes. Proc Eng 182:157–164
Forkuor D, Agyemang S (2018) Fighting urban poverty in Ghana: the role of non-governmental organizations. Urban forum. Springer, Netherlands, pp 127–145
Fronek P, Common R, Rotabi KS, Statham J (2019) Identifying and addressing risk in the implementation of alternative care policies in Cambodia. J Human Rights Soc Work 4(2):140–144
Gill T, Ricciardi V, Bates R, James D (2017) Capacity development in agricultural education and training in Cambodia: A SWOT analysis. J Int Agric Extension Educ 24(1):15–34
Haapala J, Keskinen M (2018) Influence of different discourses on the outcomes of development policies and projects: insights from water project implementation in Nepal. Environ Policy Governance 28(3):141–152
Harms H (2017) Challenges for sustainable development of informal settlements and of desert new towns in Cairo. Revitalizing city districts. Springer, Cham, pp 147–169
Ji HG (2018) The evolution of the policy environment for climate change migration in Bangladesh: competing narratives, coalitions and power. Dev Policy Rev 37(5):603–620
Kloster MO (2019) Why it hurts–Save the children Norway and the dilemmas of 'going global.' Forum for development studies. Routledge, London, pp 109–130
Markopoulos E, Aggarwal V, Vanharanta H (2019) Democratization of intrapreneurship and corporate entrepreneurship within the McKinsey's three horizons innovation space. International conference on human systems engineering and design: future trends and applications. Springer, Cham, pp 1007–1017
Martinez DE, Cooper DJ (2017) Assembling international development: accountability and the disarticulation of a social movement. Acc Organ Soc 63:6–20
McEvoy P, Brady M, Munck R (2016) Capacity development through international projects: a complex adaptive systems perspective. Int J Manag Proj Bus 9(3):528–545
Munawar NA (2019) Cultural heritage and the Arab spring: a review of international efforts to safeguard heritage under fire. The world community and the Arab Spring. Palgrave Macmillan, Cham, pp 83–115
Nhapi TG (2019) Innovating from the grassroots: perspectives constraints and opportunities of development innovation in Zimbabwe. Soc Work Policy Stud Soc Justice Pract Theor 2(1).
Noh JE (2018) The legitimacy of development nongovernmental organizations as global citizenship education providers in Korea. Educ Citizensh Soc Justice 14(3):241–259
Oliver-Smith A (2019) Disasters and large-scale population dislocations: international and national responses. Oxford Research Encyclopedia of Natural Hazard Science
Penn H (2019) Patronage, welfare, tenders, private consultancies and expert measurement: what is happening in early childhood education and care. Early childhood and development work. Palgrave Macmillan, Cham, pp 1–15
Project Management Institute (PMI) (2017) The project management body of knowledge (PMBOK® Guide). Project Management Institute Inc., PA
Rudnick J, Niles M, Lubell M, Cramer L (2019) Agricultural development networks in 14 research sites: findings from the CCAFS Organizational Baseline Survey
Saleh FIM, Karia N (2020) Benchmarks for INGOs' effective responses during COVID-19 pandemic. Benchmarking Int J 27(10):2863–2886
Saleh FI, Karia N (2022) Adaptive project management model for the international development and aid projects. Nonprofit Manag Leadersh 33(2):383–409
Saleh FIM, Sweis RJ, Abdelqader BY, Abdallah AB, Arafeh M (2017) The effect of TQM dimensions on the performance of international non-governmental organizations operating in Jordan. Int J Prod Qual Manag 21(4):443–459

Schulenkorf N (2017) Managing sport-for-development: reflections and outlook. Sport Manag Rev 20(3):243–251
Tang L (2019) Mechanism innovation for poverty alleviation and development & precise poverty alleviation. The evolution of China's poverty alleviation and development policy (2001–2015). Springer, Singapore, pp 107–135
United Nations (2019) Sustainable development goals. https://www.un.org/sustainabledevelopment/sustainable-development-goals/
Vahanvati M, Mulligan M (2017) A new model for effective post-disaster housing reconstruction: lessons from Gujarat and Bihar in India. Int J Proj Manag 35(5):802–817
Wildeman J (2017) Undermining the democratic process: the Canadian government suppression of Palestinian development aid projects. Can J Middle East Stud 2(1):2033
Zapp M (2019) International organizations, educational development, and conflict: a (world) cultural perspective. Prospects 47:321–337

Chapter 11
Management of Information for the New Normal and Sustainability

11.1 Introduction

The global pandemic of COVID-19 proved that international development outcomes can be threatened, and in turn, communities and countries can become vulnerable at any point in time. This is applied to the agency, relational, and structural levels of different kinds of entities and systems alike. Therefore, past international development investments have been questioned concerning their sustainability and their ability to deal with such major global sudden stops, which affected business continuity and even the collapse and decay of some entities and already existing systems. Particularly those that are not equipped with the required resilience capacities to survive.

Information and communications technology (ICT) readiness has been widely acknowledged as an essential capacity for resilience and sustainability alike. Not only for ensuring the business continuity of IDAPs during the COVID-19 pandemic (Saleh and Karia 2020) or supporting the readiness for disaster risk reduction (Nhamo and Eloff 2021), but also for supporting the achievement of most of the Sustainable Development Goals (Muktar et al. 2018; Ariyarathna et al. 2023). Therefore, this chapter aims to provide both theoretical and practical considerations for managing information in IDAPs, which can be used as a working framework for governing information management in both emergency and development interventions.

As the author of this book, I used to work as a senior management team member for one of the major INGOs that was operating in the Middle East during the COVID-19 pandemic and witnessed the sudden stopping of its operations that aimed to respond to the basic needs of the most vulnerable people. As such, I am currently leading the largest USAID program that aims to improve the resilience of Jordanian MSEs and put them on a path of growth. Therefore, we will provide a framework for managing the data life cycle in IDAPs and complement it with the provision of some practical strategies that can be adopted and integrated into the management of IDAPs in the interest of people of concern. This includes information provision and awareness

F. I. Mahmoud Saleh and N. Karia, *Value-driven Management for International Development and Aid Projects*, https://doi.org/10.1007/978-981-97-3666-9_11

raising, case management and psychosocial support, distribution of cash assistance, and training programs. Then, we unpacked some risks and concerns that can emerge from the adoption of ICT for delivering these programmatic components. Next, we discussed the newly appearing AI tools, including their potential applications in the IDAPs as well as their associated risks. Lastly, we concluded this chapter by providing the required processes to deal with information management as an integral part of the overall planning and management of IDAPs.

11.2 Information Management Lifecycle

Major INGOs typically have their own responsible data management and protection policies, which are informed by relevant standards and regulations, such as the EU General Data Protection Regulations (GDPR). Similarly, most international donors have their own guidelines for responsible data management, which are specified as part of the cooperative agreements and contracts with the implementing INGOs. These guidelines must be adhered to and followed when handling data collected or produced by the interventions of IDAPs.

Despite the contractual-level obligations concerning data management, IDAPs still need to have practical frameworks or protocols to operationalize these contractual obligations and reflect them in their day-to-day activities. Additionally, to express their commitment to the use of data for informing monitoring, evaluation, accountability, learning, programmatic decision-making, and adaptive management alike (Sweis et al. 2016). Furthermore, to define the information requirements, to ensure that the right information reaches the right stakeholders at the right time, and to define the procedures, roles, and responsibilities of all staff members and stakeholders concerning information management.

This section outlines a customized Data Management Lifecycle (DML) as adopted by several major INGOs like CARE International and Mercy Corps, and that can be the building blocks for the IM Protocol for IDAPs. The proposed DML encompasses design and planning, collection and acquisition, cleaning, transmission and storage, analysis and utilizing, sharing, and retention and destruction (see Fig. 11.1).

11.2.1 Design and Plan

The design and planning stage of DML aims to determine why and what data the IDAP needs, how to manage that data across the data lifecycle, and whether and how data will be treated. Therefore, the design and plan phases are about ensuring that data collection within the project has well-defined programmatic purposes and needs.

To achieve the main goal of this stage, the IDAP should depend on an information management system as a foundational platform and/or a set of electronic data

Fig. 11.1 Data management lifecycle

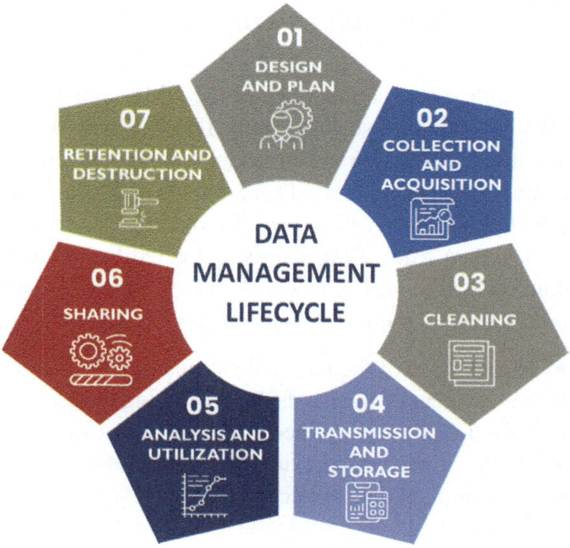

collection, analysis, and visualization tools to design data management tools. This, therefore, is to assist IDAP's teams in identifying the required data for implementing and reporting activities. Furthermore, data collection forms can be tailored to meet the evolving needs of interventions.

The design and plan for information management should be responsive to the implementation needs of the IDAPs. To that end, the IM protocol should be revised regularly in line with the updated implementation plans as well as the MEL plans. This includes identifying relevant indicators and data required to meet the contractual requirements and learning aims, such as building tools for the annual and quarterly assessments, baseline assessments, and program evaluations. Based on that, the procedures for designing and planning IDAP's information can include, but are not limited to:

- Review the implementation plans and MEL plans and unpack their activities.
- Design the data collection tools and identify the data points to be collected.
- Develop or deploy the designed data collection tools using the adopted information management system or electronic tools.
- Pilot the data collection tools.
- Train the enumerators on data collection, data collection tools, and any relevant accountability and protection measures that should be considered during the data collection.

With each procedure or action, the IM protocol should identify the roles and responsibilities, timeframes, and justification for undertaking this procedure or action. This, however, can be done in a table format to ease understanding and readability.

11.2.2 Collection and Acquisition

The Collect or Acquire stage of the DML aims to gather the data determined in the "Design and Plan" stage. Usually, IDAP collects data from various sources. However, a unified information management system or electronic tools should be used as much as possible to avoid any discrepancies and to have unified validation measures for the ultimate quality of the collected data.

The data from IDAP can be collected for several purposes, and in turn, several data collection tools can be adopted. The data collection tools can include, but are not limited to, the following:

- Registration of the targeted entities.
- Assessment of the needs or prioritizing the targeted entities.
- Submission of assistance or service provided.
- Verification of the provided services and targeted entities.
- MEL-related data collection.
- Research and programmatic assessments.
- Other programmatic data collection.

This stage of the DML entails the identification of the required consent forms for collecting data. Furthermore, it entails the automation of any adopted selection criteria for shortlisting targeted entities to ensure accountability and value-added targeting.

11.2.3 Clean

The clean stage of the DML aims to organize and prepare data for storage, transmission, analysis, and use. The information management system and tools should be able and designed to limit the possibility of incomplete and invalid data by adding mandatory and data-type constraints where possible.

To that end, IDAP's staff should coordinate and work as needed with the information management team to regularly check the validity of the data and apply the needed adjustments to incomplete and inaccurate data. Furthermore, the information management team cleans and standardizes data by identifying inconsistencies, errors, and missing values within the data, ensuring that the information collected is accurate and reliable.

The information management team can take several measures to clean up data. Each of these measures should be identified by the IM Protocol along with the roles and responsibilities, timing, and rationale behind these actions, knowing that the responsibility for generating clean data belongs to everyone. These measures can include, but are not limited to:

- **Error prevention**: such as training program staff before starting to use platforms and data collection tools.

- **Data cleaning**: to eliminate any unintended or duplicate information and complete missing information.
- **Unify and streamline data across the different data collection entry points and tools**: to ensure that all collected data from the different sources or using the different data collection tools are streamlined.
- **Regular data checks and reviews:** to check the completeness, consistency, and validity of entered data in the information management systems and databases.
- **Data correction:** includes responding to requests for correcting certain already entered data. However, this should be done using an agreed-upon process and approvals.
- **Tracking**: to preserve the original data before cleaning, and track the changes made during the cleaning process to ensure transparency in modification history, and to be ready for future tracking and data quality assessments.
- **Data quality report**: used to assess and ensure the accuracy, completeness, and validity of data. It helps identify issues for timely corrections to enhance overall data quality, contributing to reliable data for decision-making processes, continuously assessing the quality of the data, and highlighting gaps and issues for continuous improvement.

11.2.4 Transmit and Store

The transmit or store stage of the DML is about sending the data or putting it into storage. The storage of the data should be only electronic, with the limitation of paper data collection as much as possible (Sweis et al. 2016). The adopted information management system, therefore, provides a prominent level of access management, login credentials, and security permissions on various levels in integrating the data from different sources.

To ensure the protection of program participants' data, the following protection measures take place in the automation platforms adopted by the IDAP:

- **User account and password access**: the administrator of the information management system should provide each authorized user with an account username and initial password. The passwords should be enforced to be changed by the IM team or when the users request the change. User accounts should be assigned based on a particular position or role. User accounts are not to be exchanged, shared, or transferred between personnel at any time.
- **User inactivity**: the user account for personnel who have left IDAP should be locked or deactivated by the IM team and can be handled as part of the handover or clearance process.
- **Confidentiality**: the confidentiality of the participants' information must be highly respected. Only relevant information will be shared outside the IDAP (ex: an external organization) for referral or service provision to the program participants after receiving formal approval from a senior management team member.

Moreover, the internal sharing of program information should be done through the information management system, official emails, or any other electronic means.
- **Permissions**: permissions to access the information management systems should be managed centrally by the IM team in coordination with the head of quality or MEL department or team, each according to their roles and specific programmatic requirements.

11.2.5 Analyze and Use

Analyzing and using the data is about transforming it into information and knowledge for sense-making and decision-making with various stakeholders. This, however, can involve automated or manual processing via data analysis and visualization tools.

The IM team should develop and regularly maintain various automated reports and dashboards that are directly updated based on the data collected and cleaned, which makes data available and presented in user-friendly formats to cover reporting and programmatic needs. These automated tools should be designed to meet the disaggregated and contractual requirements of donors as well to inform the different levels of decision-making and various program needs. The development of automated data analytics tools should be a continuous duty.

The automated tools and dashboards can include, but are not limited to:

- Dashboards for demographic data and profiles of reached entities to ensure the required fair, relevant, and inclusive targeting.
- Dashboards for the baseline and assessment data to ensure needs-based or opportunity-based intervention design and targeting.
- Dashboards for progress reporting and key performance indicators. It is to be used as a basis for contractual reporting and IDAP's performance reviews alike.
- Dashboards for any other programmatic or research datasets undertaken under the IDAP or any other relevant published data.

11.2.6 Share

Given the multiplicity, diversity, and intersectionality of IDAP's stakeholders, interventions, and needs for data, IDAP should adopt agreed-upon procedures for data access and sharing. This section of the IM Protocol, therefore, first identifies IDAP's stakeholders, their data requirements, timing and formats of data sharing, justification for accessing and sharing data, and roles and responsibilities for regular and pre-agreed-upon data sharing: The things that can be done through the development of an information-sharing management plan. The following structure can be used for an information-sharing plan for each stakeholder:

Information	Who to share with whom?	When to share?	Why and how to share?
.			

11.2.7 *Retention and Destruction*

This phase of DML involves deciding whether and how long to retain and when and how to delete data. Usually, the IDAP retains its produced data and the data about its program participants and activities until the end of the project to facilitate implementation and management of the project. It is used for any internal or donor-led auditing and data quality assessments.

IDAPs should have the right to remove their program participants' data in the following cases, as should be identified by the IM Protocol:

1. **Incomplete or Incorrect Data**: The IDAP can delete any incomplete or incorrect data for program participants for a certain and pre-identified timeframe without reaching the owner of the data. Particularly, the data submitted by the program participants themselves, such as the wide reach or registration data.
2. **Program Participants Request**: The IDAP and its IM Protocol should guarantee the right to erasure ("*right to be forgotten*"), allowing data subjects to request the deletion of their data using a Data Deletion Request Form. The IDAP may delete primary data like names and phone numbers while retaining services in the archive for audit purposes.
3. **Determinations of the Data Management Policies**: The implementing INGO can delete any identifiable data after the end of the IDAPs according to its Responsible Data Management Policies.

11.3 Complementary Practical Information Management Strategies for IDAPs

In the past decades, the paradigm of moving thinking ways, working approaches, and modalities from one industry to another has been the dominant characteristic of the knowledge revolution, leading to many breakthroughs in various industries. Similar to any other industry, international development can be influenced by the emergence of new technologies, operational management methods, and technical practices. This applies to the emergence of global socio-economic events and even crises.

This thinking paradigm was evidently embraced by numerous scholars and practitioners. For instance, Sweis et al. (2016) advocated the applicability of the TQM approach and its practices in the INGOs industry, and therefore, they articulated their TQM Benchmarking Model for INGOs based on the TQM practices of the for-profits. However, Saleh and Karia (2020) have formulated benchmarks that INGOs can consider recovering from the sudden stopping of operations learned from the COVID-19 pandemic. To that end, they adopted McKinsey's model for organizational growth as a methodological model to solve a problem in the INGOs industry.

The IDAPs-related literature has witnessed several adoptions and adaptations to advance management practices and operations in several disciplines for the benefit of this industry. Such as but not limited to balanced scorecards (Wangu 2015), accountability and governance (Lekorwe and Mpabanga 2007), improving service quality (Fadzli Ahmad Tajuddin and Zamberi Ahmad 2013), work-related attitudes (Karia and Saleh 2021), the applicability of excellence models (Al-Tabbaa et al. 2013), project management (Saleh and Karia 2022), and corporate responsibility (Hogan 2010). Likewise, borrowing information technology practices from various industries to IDAPs is also a key manifestation of the moving thinking in this industry.

Information and Communication Technology (ICT) readiness for targeted populations, businesses, and countries is a core capacity for improving the resilience of these entities. Therefore, IDAPs should assess the needs of their targeted entities concerning this capacity and integrate such a kind of support wherever it is applicable to the activities of IDAPs. This consideration of the targeted support, however, is insufficient. IDAPs should also explore the opportunities of adopting information management tools in the implementation modalities and delivery of their added-value support.

The application areas of ICT are varying and continuously emerging. However, in the remainder of this section, we highlight some specific technical areas with the potential to leverage and utilize information management tools based on our experiences with the new COVID-19 and its new normal, refugee responses, and development programming.

11.3.1 Information Provision and Awareness Raising

Most of the IDAPs that aim to respond to emergencies and crises involve a fundamental component to improve access to specific information for their target entities. For example, refugees or displaced persons will need to be well-informed and aware of available services, service providers, legal information, updates on their original countries and areas, as well as integration and resettlement options, and more. Likewise, the IDAPs are tasked with responding to their targeted communities in the event of the spread of infectious diseases and pandemics. In this case, the need for information about health measures and vaccinations is essential. The same applies to development programming as well. Such as the IDAPs that aim to raise the awareness of their targeted micro and small private sector enterprises and home-based businesses regarding formalization, licensing, business incubators and accelerators, and access to finance.

With the increased use of technologies and the Internet of Things, most INGOs and IDAPs abandoned the traditional use of paper information provision and awareness-raising materials and relied on ICT modalities to provide information to their communities; this includes a wide spectrum of push and pull communications, such as SMSs, utilizing social media platforms, and information portals, with the integration of infographics and videography.

Utilizing these means is not only good for reaching the highest number of targeted people. But also, it is the preferred channel by those targeted people themselves, as we learned as practitioners from several multi-country field assessments. However, IDAPs must be aware that using electronic information provision and awareness might entail a risk of data protection and the exclusion of certain groups, such as children, elderly people, and people with disabilities. Therefore, using these means should be preceded by an assessment of responsible data management, inclusion, and preferences of information provision channels. For instance, according to one of our field assessments, we found that each age group, gender, or country usually has different preferences for social media platforms. Despite our discussion of this aspect under communication with the community in Chapter 8, the managers of IDAPs should also be aware of it when using ICT for information provision or raising awareness.

Using ICT for information provision has further benefits that are related to sustainability, promoting green practices, and reducing waste (Karia and Saleh 2023).

11.3.2 Case Management and Psychosocial Support

Case management is an essential bundle of services that is essential for supporting affected families in both man-made crises and natural disasters. It involves an in-depth assessment of families' needs, referral to service providers, and long-term follow-ups toward meeting emerging families' needs holistically.

During the COVID-19 pandemic, I worked for an INGO that quickly transitioned its case management services from in person to over the phone and video calls, utilizing a call center for this purpose. As movement restrictions were lifted and life returned to normal, we considered making this virtual modality a permanent part of our services after the pandemic while also returning to face-to-face interactions. This decision came after discussions and consultations with targeted households and technical teams. The goal is to reduce transportation costs for vulnerable households and ensure that people with specific needs are not left behind. This approach also allows case managers to meet all members of families, observe, and address any gender dynamics or gender-based violence risks. That said, most beneficiaries stated their preference for discussing sensitive issues, such as cases of sexual and gender-based violence, in person rather than over the phone.

The same discussion has been held about our psychosocial support services. We developed multimedia content and pushed it to our targeted beneficiaries via social media platforms and mobile phones. While this approach has been supported to be adopted as part of our new normal to match the needs of caregivers and the entailed flexibility, psychosocial support serves as a return to its original in-person modality based on the psychosocial specialists, as they indicated the risk of dealing with severe psychological cases remotely as it might be negatively perceived by these groups.

11.3.3 Distribution of Cash Assistance

Cash-based assistance is one of the key modalities used by IDAPs to support vulnerable people during crisis times to give flexibility in managing their purchases. Likewise, it is one of the main modalities for nexus and development programming to support businesses, community-based organizations, and local entities through the provision of monetary grants to advance their missions.

The distribution of cash assistance during crises and emergencies can be logistically challenging or even impossible. Such as the cases where the operations of humanitarian actors and INGOs are not allowed or are surrounded by severe safety and security risks. Using electronic means in such cases, therefore, will be irreplaceable. As such, it might be adopted intentionally in some cases related to healthcare measures and gender-based violence to target girls and women who might be negatively impacted by receiving cash through traditional means. Key modalities might include electronic transfers to local exchangers or using electronic wallets to transfer cash to the programs' participants. Accordingly, INGOs should have already established technological means and local partnerships as part of their operational preparedness for emergency responses.

In the context of nexus and development programming, where sustainability aspects are intentionally pursued, it may be necessary to introduce digital financial services to targeted groups to enhance their financial literacy or make them bankable. Therefore, ICT technologies, like e-payments, need to be programmatically integrated into the concepts of IDAPs with value-added aims.

11.3.4 Training Programs

Training is a widely adopted modality for capacity development programs in the different contexts of IDAPs. It is used to build the capacity of different targeted entities through these projects as a cornerstone for changing behaviors, improving their capacities, affecting their attitudes, strengthening their resilience, and putting them on a path of growth. Using electronic means, however, has been widely acknowledged as an effective modality for creating training content and delivering training to impact targeted entities at scale, ensure effectiveness through reusability, and overcome barriers to attending and benefiting from in-person training. Accordingly, electronic content and online training have been intentionally adopted for several extended socio-economic and social inclusion aims of IDAPs.

The adoption of virtual training has evolved dramatically because of the global COVID-19 pandemic, its associated curfews, prohibition of gatherings, and movement restrictions. Whereas most INGOs around the globe have switched their training programs to this modality and further adopted it as a permanent strategy for the reasons mentioned above (Saleh and Karia 2020).

Despite the wide spectrum of benefits, online content, and virtual training, these modalities can entail several concerns and risks, as follows:

- **Exclusion Risks**: The IDAPs who adopt this modality should be aware of the lack of accessibility for some people with specific needs, genders, or age groups to training programs. Therefore, they should make sure to equip their platforms with the required accessibility options. This is to make sure that the interactive sessions are conducted at suitable times for caregivers and working parents.
- **Social Concerns**: According to our field observations, we have witnessed several dropouts and refusals of participation in the interactive virtual training sessions because these sessions mixed different gender groups in the same session. This can be a particular concern for some communities, such as refugee camps that host people from conservative communities. Therefore, the adoption of e-modalities for training programs should be preceded by a gender analysis to inform the design and delivery of these programs to the targeted groups.
- **Affordability**: While the adoption of virtual training is an effective modality for IDAPs to reduce costs and reach the highest number of entities, as it can save the logistical costs and the time as well as the cost of transportation to reach the training venues, it can also add further costs for the targeted people. Using the Internet in developing or crisis-affected countries might be costly for some of the communities and vulnerable people. Therefore, IDAPs should consider paying reasonable costs for internet bundles for their targeted groups while making sure that these costs or the internet are not perceived or treated as an aim by themselves. This is particularly important in emergencies and targeting vulnerable people, but not in development contexts.
- **Accountability Concerns**: IDAPs are always required to provide evidence for their implemented activities and reached targets. While this might be easy to verify in the in-person training programs by collecting attendance sheets, signatures, and photos, it might be difficult to do the virtual training. Therefore, IDPAs should ensure the availability of measures and means to ensure verification of implemented activities and ultimate accountability to their donors. This might include recording training sessions and e-signatures, along with the attendance of M&E teams at some of these sessions as part of the internal M&E systems of the IDAPs and implementing INGOs.

11.4 Artificial Intelligence (AI) and IDAPs

Like for-profit organizations, INGOs and IDAPs can benefit from any continuously emerging technologies to advance their missions in different directions. For instance, they can adopt these technologies externally to analyze the trends of their current and potential donors and the needs of their targeted populations. Likewise, they can adopt these technologies to improve their internal operations. Such as analyzing their data, writing reports, and producing different kinds of operational deliverables. However, when it comes to interacting with vulnerable people and targeted groups, IDAPs should be fully aware of several opportunities and risks.

Artificial Intelligence (AI) is a newly emerged technology that has become widely used across all industries. In 2023, I participated in training on well-known qualitative data collection software. At the end of the workshops, I asked the trainer if we could use AI applications to analyze our collected data. Her response was direct and clear, stating that these applications entail a high risk concerning the data protection of targeted people. Three months later, the same trainer, who worked as a global advisor in our INGO, sent us an update that the company that developed this software has added and released an AI add-on to this software package.

In the same week, I received demo software from one of the ICT companies that developed software that uses AI technology to translate surveys into human-like avatars that ask the survey questions in an automated way by sending a link to the mobile phones of respondents. Furthermore, this ICT company has shared with us a list of NGOs that have started using their software in their data collection activities.

During the past month of writing this chapter, we received a request for a grant from one of the startups that aim to develop software that uses AI to bridge the digital divide for our targeted Micro and Small Enterprises (MSEs), transforming local obscurity into online success. Their intended tools and AI-powered optimization aim to propel MSEs into new e-commerce markets, boosting visibility, customer engagement, and sales through analyzing product information, pinpointing missing content, and suggesting adjustments for optimal online visibility across multiple e-commerce channels.

Such progress, which I witnessed as a practitioner, can indicate the inevitability of adopting AI applications in this industry, whether we agree or not. Therefore, INGOs should accept this fact and even be proactive in identifying opportunities to benefit from this emerging technology and add value to their IDAPs, while keeping a close eye on the risks associated with adopting such technology among their targeted groups.

In addition to the proven cross-industrial benefits, the opportunities and added-value applications related to the adoption of AI can be summarized as follows:

- **Data collection**: using AI for data collection, however, is particularly worthy of being considered as an effective way in cases of huge data collection, a lack of resources, overcoming any logistical barriers to reaching targeted respondents, and during emergencies.

- **Data analysis and visualization**: using AI for data analysis and visualization is a key benefit of using this continuously developed technology. Such as visualization of trends and results of research in very short timeframes, which can save efforts and resources.
- **Targeting and prioritization of support**: with the lack of funding faced by IDAPs, these projects are always under pressure to prioritize their support for the most vulnerable entities. Therefore, AI can play a vital role in analyzing the results of needs assessments, market assessments, and gender assessments to identify gaps, intersectionality, and the neediest groups for the assistance and support of IDAPs in both emergency and development contexts.
- **Evaluation of IDAPs**: identification of the intended and unintended impacts of IDAPs is one of the most challenging pieces of work for these complex projects. This is in addition to the lack of quality individual and organizational competencies to undertake such tasks, which can result in misleading or missed identification of IDAPs' impacts. Getting what human eyes cannot capture from the cross-cutting impacts of IDAPs, therefore, can be one of the most important applications of this technology in this industry.

In contrast, the adoption of AI can be fraught with risks and warnings that should be aware of and critically assessed before deciding to proceed, particularly when dealing with externally owned AI platforms and tools. These risks and warnings can include, but are not limited to:

- **Data protection**: as mentioned earlier in this chapter, responsible data management is a key requirement for donors and INGOs when dealing with the data of targeted people. Therefore, IDAPs leaders should ensure that their staff are fully aware and do not upload any personally identifiable information to the external AI platforms. This, furthermore, should be associated with strict and deterrent punitive measures to deal with any breaches in this regard.
- **Hallucination of AI**: it means incorrect predictions, in which AI might produce invalid conclusions that appear as facts to the users, while they are not. This, therefore, might be harmful to the affected people in terms of making incorrect assumptions or even decisions about their situation, needs, and opportunities.
- **Loss of human interaction**: one of the key missions of INGOs is to intermediate the role between donors and targeted entities. Therefore, to benefit from their expertise and acceptance, assistance and support will be delivered to them. The same applies to the IDAPs that traditionally aim to operationalize the strategies of donors and INGOs and translate them into added-value realities for the lives and capacities of those entities. Regardless of what these entities are, human interaction is still a key to delivering quality outcomes. This aim, however, can be lost in the case of over-adoption of AI tools, which in turn undermines these aims. Accordingly, IDAPs are required to ensure that their human and direct interaction is always maintained.

11.5 Project Management Processes for Information Management

The use of quality information includes the availability of timely and accurate information about targeted entities and the implementation progress of IDAPs alike. Sweis et al. (2016) have emphasized the importance of accessing the inter-agency information management platforms and their reporting requirements as part of their TQM-benchmarking model. Likewise, they have indicated that the primary data of IDAPs should be collected through modern data collection tools as a manifestation of this model. Information management has proven itself a helpful tool to be harnessed within IDAPs as part of the overall accountability and the interests of vulnerable entities and their needs (Camacho et al. 2019; Robehmed 2019; Kaba 2019).

To that end, Saleh and Karia (2020) have raised the following questions for managing IDAPs concerning information management:

- How to ensure the availability of information on targeted groups that can inform assistance and targeting decisions?
- How can the personal data of targeted people be protected?
- How to ensure quality collection, availability, timeliness, accuracy, and well-dissemination of implementation and progress?
- How to ensure constant data collection using modern technology?
- How to ensure adequate access to and maintenance of inter-agency and coordination information management systems?

Therefore, they critiqued the available project management standards in terms of their ability to cover the need for having an information management plan and, in turn, meet the needs of IDAPs in this regard.

To cover this gap, Saleh and Karia (2022) proposed to consider the development of an "*information management plan*" as part of their proposed project management process of "*Plan MEAL*." This information management plan, which is considered a subsidiary plan of the MEAL Framework, aims to identify the policies and procedures, and guidance for dealing with sensitive beneficiary information, to identify data collection tools, analysis, and visualization, and to work in line with the communication management and stakeholder management processes to ensure fair availability of project information and progress for all stakeholders based on the results framework or logframes of IDAPs. They also indicated the importance of considering the risk of illegal access to beneficiary data as one of the risk categories dealt with when identifying the risks of these projects.

References

Al-Tabbaa O, Gadd K, Ankrah S (2013) Excellence models in the non-profit context: strategies for continuous improvement. Int J Qual & Reliab Manag 30(5):590–612

Ariyarathna SK, Nanayakkara KGM, Thushara SC (2023) The nexus of farmers' sustainable agriculture potential and readiness for more organic use in rice farming: insights from resilience theory. Sustain Environ 9(1):2273619
Fadzli Ahmad Tajuddin A, Zamberi Ahmad S (2013) Impact of environmental scanning on the organisational performance of local authorities in Malaysia. TGPPP 7(3):342–363
Hogan E (2010) Does 'corporate' responsibility apply to not-for-profit organizations? Professionals' perspectives of corporate social responsibility, pp 271–288
Karia N, Saleh FIM (2021) The effect of TQM practices on INGOs' staff work-related attitudes. Benchmarking: Int J 29(2):596–621
Karia N, Saleh FIM (2023) Hajj management chain feasibility post COVID-19. In: Prospects and challenges of global pilgrimage tourism and hospitality. IGI Global, pp 83–95
Lekorwe M, Mpabanga D (2007) Managing non-governmental organizations in Botswana. Innov J: Public Sect Innov J 12(3):1–18
Muktar BG, Man N, Kamaruzzaman NH, Samah AA, Umar S (2018) Fishers ICTs use for early warning reception, it's effect on livelihood resilience and sustainability in east coast Malaysia. J Agric VetY Sci 11(1):63–72
Nhamo G, Eloff MM (2021) ICT readiness for disaster risk reduction: lessons from tropical cyclone Idai. In: Cyclones in Southern Africa: Volume 2: foundational and fundamental topics. Springer, pp 87–103
Saleh FIM, Karia N (2020) Benchmarks for INGOs' effective responses during COVID-19 pandemic. Benchmarking: Int J 27(10):2863–2886
Saleh FIM, Karia N (2022) Adaptive project management model for the international development and aid projects. Nonprofit Manag Leadersh 33(2):383–409
Sweis RJ, Saleh FIM, Dahiyat SE, Sweis NJ, Saleh RA, Diab H (2016) Benchmarking of TQM practices in INGOs: A literature review. Benchmarking: Int J 23(1):236–261
Wangu DK (2015) Balanced score card and performance of non governmental organizations in Kenya. Doctoral dissertation

GPSR Compliance

The European Union's (EU) General Product Safety Regulation (GPSR) is a set of rules that requires consumer products to be safe and our obligations to ensure this.

If you have any concerns about our products, you can contact us on ProductSafety@springernature.com

In case Publisher is established outside the EU, the EU authorized representative is:

Springer Nature Customer Service Center GmbH
Europaplatz 3
69115 Heidelberg, Germany

The manufacturer's authorised representative in the EU is Springer Nature Customer Service Centre GmbH, Europaplatz 3, 69115 Heidelberg, Germany. If you have any concerns regarding our products, please contact ProductSafety@springernature.com

Printed and bound by CPI Group (UK) Ltd, Croydon, CR0 4YY
30/09/2026
02225309-0013